T0196623

Come Lemme Hea' Yoh Yank Soursap

clement white

authorHOUSE®

AuthorHouse™
1663 Liberty Drive
Bloomington, IN 47403
www.authorhouse.com
Phone: 1 (800) 839-8640

© 2017 clement white. All rights reserved.

No part of this book may be reproduced, stored in a retrieval system, or transmitted by any means without the written permission of the author.

Cover Photography by Shirlene Williams Lee

Published by AuthorHouse 12/20/2017

ISBN: 978-1-5462-1894-4 (sc)
ISBN: 978-1-5462-1893-7 (hc)
ISBN: 978-1-5462-1892-0 (e)

Library of Congress Control Number: 2017918156

Print information available on the last page.

Any people depicted in stock imagery provided by Thinkstock are models, and such images are being used for illustrative purposes only. Certain stock imagery © Thinkstock.

This book is printed on acid-free paper.

Because of the dynamic nature of the Internet, any web addresses or links contained in this book may have changed since publication and may no longer be valid. The views expressed in this work are solely those of the author and do not necessarily reflect the views of the publisher, and the publisher hereby disclaims any responsibility for them.

Contents

PART II

For

Mrs. Viola Simmonds, "Moms," mentor, guide, surrogate mother
Butty, who elevated the art of storytelling
Corey Emmanuel and *Lezmore Emmanuel*, trailblazers—Virgin Islands guardians of culture and history, true Ashanti poets and griots

The strong, resourceful, and resilient residents of the Virgin Islands, US and British, who endured the wrath of a relentless Irma and the ire of a defiant María

IN LOVING MEMORY

MARJORIE-MARGARITA ASTA WHITE STEVENS—
JEANNETTE SMITH WHITE —NEVER ENDING LOVE

—MY LOVING SIBLINGS: LEILA, KEITH, ELDRIDGE, REOVAN
(CORDELL)—MUCH LOVE

MENTORS

—MR. RALPH V. SIMMONDS…MRS. VIOLA L. SIMMONDS
—CHRISTALIA "MISS CHRISSY" TESTAMARK
—CELESTINE "MISS CELES" TURNBULL
—MR. VALDEMIR HILL….MRS. FLORENCE HILL

For my Virgin Gorda family, especially Hilda and Iris—images of my mother, MARJORIE-MARGARITA ASTA WHITE STEVENS—

For my St. Croix family, images of my Father, CHARLES ALEXANDER WHITE

REMEMBERING MY MOTHER, **MARJORIE ASTA WHITE STEVENS**; MY FATHER, **CHARLES ALEXANDER WHITE, SR.** MY LOVING AUNTS & UNCLE IN GROVE, FREDERIKSTED, LA VALLEE:

Auntie Vivian "Cooley" Acoy, Auntie Florence "Flory" Austin, Auntie Lillian Bailey, Uncle William "Willie" Carrol, Auntie Miriam King, Auntie Rhoda Senthill

The poet's eye, in a fine frenzy rolling,
Doth glance from heaven to earth, from earth to heaven;
And as imagination bodies forth
The forms of things unknown, the poet's pen
Turns them to shapes and gives to aery nothing
A local habitation and a name.

William Shakespeare, <u>A Midsummer Night's Dream</u>, Act V, I, 12-17

Acknowledgements

Endless thanks to my wife, Dr. Jeannette Smith White, who continues to inspire me. I benefited from her constant input in all of my works. To our children, Sekou "Chike" and Asha, grandsons, Amari and Ahsir, and granddaughter Avani ("mi princesa") you mean the world to me. Thanks to my mother, Marjorie Margarita "Miss Maggie" White Stevens for uncompromising, unconditional support; now even as her work on earth was ended on October 10, 2014, I know that she will continue to guide and inspire me; so remarkable a mother, woman, and human being she was. She never attended school, never read a book, but was my most important teacher. Ana Cecilia Rosado I appreciate our years of friendship. To Marta Rodríguez Galán, thanks for many years of support.

To my sister Cheryl A. White, because of your dedication to our mother, I was able to continue writing. I recognize and appreciate your sacrifice and dedication to our beloved mother. What you have meant to our family can never be captured in words. Your diligence and commitment were noteworthy. Your rewards will be great!

To fellow and sister writers Habib Tiwoni, Dr. Gilbert Sprauve, Elaine Warren Jacobs, Dr. Vincent Cooper, Daisy Holder, Dr. Ruby Simmonds, Larry Sewer, Tregenza Roach and the prolific Dr. Simon B. Jones Hendrickson, Edgar Lake and Richard Scharader, you are an inspiration to all Virgin Islands writers; your works have served as literary models over the years. Edgar, you are a brilliant scholar whose advice and guidance have been instrumental in my literary career.

To my colleagues, Mario Trubiano, Susana de los Heros, and Tomás Morín. Gracias por todo el apoyo. Karla Crispín, thanks for all your technical advice and support. Dr. Alexandra Cornelius, thanks for your support of this project.

Shirlene Williams Lee from the very beginning in the 1960's you played a pivotal role in the transcription of my work, typing my manuscripts with your inimitable professionalism and expertise. Thanks for finding the most appropriate book cover, using your photographic skills, just one of your many talents. Words are not sufficient to express my gratitude to you. Critic, poet, analyst, sounding board, photographer, artist, designer, and more importantly, friend—from the first grade at the extraordinary Dober School until now! You have been there every step of the way. Everything you do, you do it well. Without your assistance this project would have never been completed.

Marilyn David, "Marilyn-Tamba" thanks for your years of friendship and discussions of Virgin Islands culture and traditions while at Kent State. Lesmore "Dandy" Howard, James "Jaime Benítez" Hedrington, Kwame "Mote" Motilewa, Justino "Tino" Colón, much thanks. Dandy, your reservoir of Virgin Islands history, culture, and traditions has no end. So much knowledge! Because of our 50+ years of friendship I have been the beneficiary of your knowledge. I consider myself lucky. My friends for life in St. Croix, Glen Byron and Deanna L. Sackey, I appreciate your friendship so much.

To all our mothers in Paul M. Pearson Gardens during the 1950's, '60's, and early 70's, who sacrificed all so that we could grow up as solid citizens, thank you so much. Miss Ruth Thomas, dedicated educator and motivator of generations of Virgin Islanders thanks. *To dem Housin' boys and guirls*, I will never forget you. Thanks for helping to mold me. Special thanks and recognition to la señora Fiolina Mills, Alicia Ortiz, Carmen Encarnación …for your many Spanish lessons in the 1960's.

Mrs. Bernice Louise Heyliger, everyone now knows that without you, I would not be writing anything. Endless thanks and appreciation.

Introduction

Several years ago I was asked in an interview about my "outline" for writing poetry, and my answer, I suppose, surprised the interviewer: "I have none, but rather I believe that my poetry responds to a call from within me, as natural as Vicente Huidobro was proposing." I vividly remember this response, recalling the Chilean's poet blueprint in his work "Poetic Art."("Arte poética,"1916). I have always felt a sense of liberation reading Huidobro and contemplating the words: *Let the verse be like a key that opens a thousand doors.* This speaks to the freedom of poetic expression, of not being enslaved to artistic protocol.

The numerous storytellers in the West Indies, are epitomized in my mind by the inimitable Butty, one of my many literary muses.* Several years have passed since **Wey Butty** and **Network of Spheres** were published, but a number of the poems in this selection were written, within two years of the publication of those works in 2003. In 2016 I had the privilege of attending a conference in La Habana Cuba, and was immediately inspired to respond to the muses in the land of José Martí and Nicolás Guillén. Verses written in Spanish are interpreted into English. The poems on Cuba are included in this collection and in **From Here to There: Uneven Steps Marking Time**.

The themes of **Come Lemme Hea' Yoh Yank Soursap** were not selected, but rather emerged themselves in the process of formulating the "verse." The use of Virgin Islands Creole always calls into question the "intent" of the author in "choosing" this medium of communication. Like everything else in this collection, I do not see this as a "choice." In the process of creating the verses, in some cases that is the style that took form; that in fact had to take form. I am sure, however, that some of my friends would argue that I did make that "choice" in order to authenticate and legitimate the *language*. These friends argue that it was an unconscious choice, a kind of antithetical formula that even I do not quite understand. At this time, however, I leave psychology to those imminently qualified to use it. I invite you to read these verses, to be my collaborative literary partner.

*Butty was a naturally gifted storyteller from St. Thomas, Virgin Islands. In the 50's & 60's he kept his audience spellbound with impeccable timing and a perfect narrative cadence. Refer to <u>Wey Butty</u>, pp. 13.

PART I

Lemme Hea' Yoh Yank Soursap
(To my brother Celestino A. White)

People leave from home to visit "deh States,"
Gone for a short while to return to these gates,
Bitin' deh tongue dey no longa' want toh say "*tain no true*"
Refuse toh say "*arm ting*" or "*me ain' in dat wid ah you*"

Now speaking differently their intonation has totally changed,
Now it is: "*please do me a favor and pass me that **Or**'ange,*"
They no longer speak of "mango," "suga' apple," or "locus"
But now say: "*oh my, what lovely fruits exist here on St. Thomas!*"

They say how one was showin' off on deh waterfront one sunny day,
Fo' 5 dollars ah fish, he Garn takin' out ah hundred dolla' bill toh pay,
Saw a fish and asked the fisherman: "*What kind of fish is that? Do say.*"
Put his hand too close then screamed out: "*Ay ya yai, deh Ole Wife bite meh!*"

According to what people say, the same man then saw a crab,
Once more, like before, he wanted to show off, wanted to brag,
Bu' how he live' in deh states and how we down heh duz speak so funny,
Say he ain know it was ah crab, geh bite, an' bawl' out': "*Squeeze he gundy!*"

One time Ah hea' dis woman yankin' on one ah dem big Pan Am plane,
Speakin' loud fo' spite she was bitin' off her tongue again and again,
Talkin' toh ha' daughta' she was yankin' up ah storm: "*See, we are quite high in the sky.*"
Den forget she ain no real Yankee and said: "*Guirl, yoh betta' si'down and res' yoh eye.*"

Man visitin' deh islands jus' after ah few weeks livin' in New York or Miami,

Don' forget where every place is, went out Grove Place and said: *"Quiet City,"*
Went to Trunk Bay and asked: *"Can one maintain his eyes opened when he dives?"*
Then fakin' come yankin' toh me: *"Fellow, on what side of the street does one drive?"*

The "states" convert our folk quickly, changing their original, local lingo,
No more "bush tea" talk, it is all about *"that backward speech called calypso,"*
They keep askin' *"Excuse me, what you say again?"* actin' like dey ain understand yoh,
Bu' we know full well dat dey haven't really forgotten their native tongue fo' true

Because when you see Virgin Islanders trying to impress you with the new fake parlance,
My brother Celestino gave me a sure way to stop them in their frenzied linguistic dance,
He told me, *"Brudda, tis really quite easy, yoh know, to set up the perfect language trap,*
Le' dem yank away, den quietly say: "Ok, Partna' now lemme hea' yoh yank **"sour sap!"**

Bethlehem Sacred Fields

(My Crucian Cousins & Glen "Jarko" Byron and Deanna Sackey)

Majestic St. Croix cane fields
You are not just ornaments
But hold deep secrets
Of sacrifice, commitment,
Fortunate was I to walk many
Of those fields, even at a time
When the lessons of history
Were not at all clear to
One so young, so naïve,
But St. Croix fields,
You still have inscribed
Deep in your soil the narrative
Of the daily strife, struggle, pain
Dedication to a future generation
Of Virgin Islanders, of West Indians
No ordinary place, these fields that
Chronicle St. Croix's rich history
Converging, at times diverging from St. John's
Which converges and diverges from
That of St. Thomas,
But all pointing to the Virgin Islands past,
St. Croix cane fields,
I remember you so well,
Looking up at the stacks of cane
That seemed to be reaching for the skies
Much like those who before tilled the fields
Looked to the HEAVENS for relief
From back breaking, dehumanizing work,

In the fields that sacredly guard
Bitter truths and diaries of real people,
Toiling to ensure a future Virgin Islands,
Cane fields of St. Croix,
Majestic, regal fields,
I thank you for initiating me
In my own innocent way to
The true lessons of the past,
I want to walk those fields again
And feel once more
The presence of the caretakers
And hear their vibrating echoes
Traversing those precious grounds
That have recorded data of my turbulent
Virgin Islands history symbolized by my St. Croix

1733 – Liberation Quest
(Dr. Gilbert Sprauve)

Revolt, Resistance,
will to be free
burning in the restless
spirits of the rebels
looking out at the Atlantic,
and the Caribbean Sea,
day-dreaming
of the Mother Country,
of invaders, kidnappers
with weapons of diplomacy,
destroyers of families
with their carbine rifles
anxious for action in the
still of the night

Africa held its stomach
in pain and was treated with high
dosage of lead,
Africa screamed
"Don't take my children"
but could only look in the distance
as the usual friend, the sea,
turned conspirator,
a major accomplice of the
tourist ships to the Virgins

Revolt, Resistance,
will to be free, St. John's

heroes and heroines summoned the
Akan spirits intertwined with their own,
St. Johnians chose dignity
over humiliation,
over subjugation
over submission
Pride over dehumanization
African Pride,
West Indian Pride
Virgin Islands Pride

Heroes of St John looked out at the
bodies of water coming together
and then themselves chose to unite,
these men and women
yearning for freedom
willed to them by the CONTINENT

Freedom fighters
tired of the whip
of the ankle decoration
of the constant human
degradation,
cried the name of freedom,
of emancipation,
with their eyes still
viewing the Caribbean Sea
with their dreams of once
again crossing the Atlantic Ocean
Resisters,
rebels *with* a cause
changed the state of slaves everywhere,
with one bold act
emanating from the womb
of the rebellious African
Continent, and

Ghana
that refused to sleep while her
children were being recast
as anti heroes

Wa' Dey Name Again?
(Cyndy Clenniden, mey cousin)

Ah meet ah man ah day in Savan who come tarkin' toh me
Say 'bou how he lookin' fo' Robert, Michael, and Randy,
Ah tell deh man Ah dain know who he wuz tarkin' 'bout
Dat's wen Ah realize dat dem real names duz cause me doubt

"Look Mista, yoh need toh change yoh tune wen yoh talk 'bout yoh friens'
'Cause Ah wan' toh hea' 'bout Shorty deh Zulu, Koka deh Bear and dem,
Tell me 'bout Tremblin' Dick, Nantern Joe, Buddy, an' he dey call Fungy
Double, Neck, Tumpa, Magoo, Seize-Up, and ah boy we duz call Tumpy"

He wuz ah man from St. Thomas who had jus' return' from New Yark
And arl deh partna' ha' wan' toh do was run he mout' an' jus' tark,
Sayin' bu' how he remember' dem ole time folk from so very larg ago,
Ah say, "yoh mean Bummin' Chow, Buzzard, School Food and Scobo?"

Ah tell deh man dat Ah ain' see dem people in years,
Man begin toh bus' arl kin' ah big crocodile tears,
I now recall some of those nicknames, he finally said
"Like Bumless, Quart Gas and this man called Heads"

"Virgin Islands nicknames are incredible," the man remarked
"You remember El Gato deh Ciat, and deh Dessert Hawk?"
Ah repeated toh the fella dat most ah dem people don' garn,
Ah tarkin' 'bout Mollet, Bloat, Ben-up, Mousy, and Rattarn.

"Bu' wa happen' toh Bunwood, Bings, an' he dey call Butty?
Wey Wa-He-Name from Garden Street an' she from country?
Tis' larng time Ah ain see dem, an' look heh, frien, 'tain me alone,

8

'Cause Ah tell yoh, mey boy, Ah duz neva'see dis man dey call Jawbone"

Ah shouted to the man: "Meson, Ah don' tell yoh many times aready
You wid arl yoh crazy question dem jus' makin' me feel so bazzidy
Dem de yoh askin' 'bout wuz arl good people dat we ha' know
Like mey boy Skianta Fat, Bumsky, an', yes, mey partna' Slimmo"

In the Virgin Islands very often you may not know a person's real name
But never worry one moment, my friend, you must not feel at all ashamed,
Because we live by the nickname, dat's ah part of deh culture fo' so
Like Rakon, Dog Bite, Deep Curve, an' ah Tutu boy name' Larko

There was this boy from Housin' we used toh call 'im Frako
An' ah good athlete from Grove Place we always call' 'im Jarko
In these islands people call you whatever they very well please
It's as if it were inherent in our nature to enjoy a good tease

Someone might call you Kako, Pound-Ah-Lip, Larng Giarlin, or Big Guts
Buck Teet, Knack Knee, Cock Eye, Bones, So' Foot, or jus' plain "Mutt,"
Partna,' doan make any kin' ah mistake o' say anyting wrang or strange
'Cause befo' yoh know it, frien', yoh birth name will suddenly change

They might rename you Hook, Squeeze-up, Ciat eye, Panty, Boom' Egg,
Fish Eye,
Flat Tap, High Beam, Scalamoosh, or some other name that at first will
make you cry,
They might call you Criminal Curls, then later shorten that nickname to
Crimmo
Or simply name yoh Bassy, Shadow, Sarge, Duke, Cabalao, Flash, or jus'
Mocko.

Be careful, someone might call yoh Borum Guts, Double Ugly, or Shango
Suck-Tongue La La, Peep Sight, or simply say *"yoh iz jus' ah Pappy Show"*
That person might be watching you closely to see what name to stick on you
Then might try Skinny Arrow, John Darg, Shoeses, Ciat Soup or settle
for Gotto

In the V.I. deh people "study yoh" the same way dey examine a text,
You see, they are trying to figure out what label to pin on you next,
They might go to the animal kingdom as the source for their latest choice,
Den en' up callin' yoh Piggy, Ducks, Monkey Meat, Lizard, or Wood Lice

Dey might prefer Horsy, Groun' Hag, Fraggie, Panta, Bull, Small Fry, or Chicken,
Or rename yoh Ciat, Dargy, Turtle, Darg Mange, Moose, or, like mey frien Snakin
Ah say, "watch yourself, yes sah, be careful with everything yoh say an' do
Because, Mista, in an instant yoh no longa', "Raymond," but officially Kuboo"

Yoh cou' hea' Frisky, Bim Bee, or like mey classmate in St. John, Sharky,
Or maybe they will call yoh Lamp, Momsie, Bun-up, Guirlie, or jus' Kitty,
Please, no mo' "Celestino," "Luben," "Edwita," Lucien," and arl dat stuff
'Cause "Start-Ova'," "Diamon'," "Tin tin," and "Red Man" would be enough

So sir, if yoh really wan toh tark, ask meh 'bout Peep-up, Buckle, Limpy, 'an Naska
But doan forget 'bout Blue, Crookéd, Ram, Peewee, an 'ah fella name Shaka
Dem is who Ah know, not arl dem Yankee name yoh come heh now busin' meh today
Man, Skip deh "right names" dem if yoh geh someting on yoh min' yoh wan' toh say

In Cruz dey had dis fella we eva' use toh call 'im by deh name Gayo,
Ask he real name, frien, an if yoh pay meh Ah really coun' tell yoh
In Grove Place mey Auntie sen' meh toh Pedro Sto' toh buy some black eye peas
By deh time Ah reach home dey chiren dem wuz done in deh mood to tease

Dey had aready change' mey name in that short trip to that well known store,
Ah fin' out dat dey name mey mudda ha' give meh was not gon be use' no more,
My name was suddenly different, my Grovians friens' did it with such ease,

Dey say Ah ask' fo deh wrang ting, so in Grove Place, I became "**Black Peas!**"

So mista' wen yoh wan' toh get in contact with someone in my isluns
Doan cum heh usin' arl kinda propa' an' fancy name toh meh, meson,
Like Edward, Darwin, Ruben, Arthur, Mary, Bill, Susan and dem ting so,
Instead tell me he name— Husky, Ducky, Red belly, Two Cent, OOks,
or Squanto

Because if you give me all those names that were used to baptize dem,
To tell the truth I would not be able to help you identify yoh friens'
But bus' meh ah Bat Ear, Crawley, Torch, 88, or he brudda, Diggie
Scohole, Joe Meat, Tootie, or ah 'roun' deh fiel' fellow named Mimie

In dat way, Secko, Ah cou' help yoh fin' who i'tis yoh really seek
Whether dey call 'im Corn Pork, Skippy, Skoompy, Devil, or Beek,
Deh man seemed very happy, he surely liked what I had said,
Claiming: "*I will never forget those people, whether living or dead*"

Then he said that before returning to New York City next day
He had to see Junka Iron, Blinky, and Gunslinger in some way,
"But Mista," I said, 'bout mos' ah dem boys Ah carn help yoh,
But Ah cou' sho' yoh way toh find *Shake-Um Peggy an' Tampo*"

Dese Rocks

Virgin Islands on sale,
Bargain prices of yesteryear,
Competing nationalities
Placing their stakes without fear
In the virgin soil
Of the volcanic rock
Formed by arbitrary
Stresses in the Caribbean land,
Subjugation, enslavement, revolt,
Rebellion
Telltale signs of human failures,
Of Virgin Islands history
Locked in closets of
Oblivion and amnesia!

Virgin Islands endured it all
Like a resilient stallion,
Islands identified by their
Rolling, majestic hills
Blue waters of the Caribbean
And the Atlantic,
Beautiful, still

Uneven boulders overlooking
The seas
Caribbean place with its hibiscus and
Flamboyant trees,
Virgin Islands, standing the
Test of time

Irma Tink She Bad

Irma followed Harvey
With more belligerence and anger,
She wan' toh upstage him,
She forwad an' saucy,
But deh people dem 'fraid
Toh tell ha',
Residents try to discourage
Her from idle competition,
Harvey greeted Houston without
Sympathy and care,
Harvey's performance was remarkable,
Heartless attacker
Feeling no empathy,
Irma "suck ha teet" an' say bu'
How she cou beat Harvey,
While the innocent begged her to
Keep her distance,
Irma shrugged supported by her
Vicious merciless winds, named
4 and 5,
The Antilles begged Irma to keep her
Safe distance,
Irma argued that it is her day
In the tropics to unpend
Scare
Uproot
Create panic,
Annihilate, when possible,
They say how she was

Screaming and creating
Diabolic sounds,
Irma wants to erase Harvey's fame
        Ah carn stan ha!
Sickening winds
Screeching, howling like ah darg,
Ah mean, like ah wolf
Irma too rude
Even Hugo, Marilyn, Bertha,
Frederick, David and dem
Say Irma too rude,
Ah yoh take ah back seat,
Deh real bad sheriff jus
Pas' tru
Guns blazing, taking
No prisoners,
Dat Irma, causing
Castrotrophic damage
An' pain in mey islun
Boy, Ah carn stan ha!!

Soul Searching
(To my brother Charles A. White)

My Savan Yard had no name
Except that used by my dear mother
Who called it simply *"Deh Yard"*
Perhaps a denomination used by the
Strong willed women like her,
The leaders and guarantors of
Happiness within the contours of
My little Savan space,
Made ever increasingly distant,
Savan, I implore you, do not disclaim me,
Since I will always claim you,
For etched in my head are those
Days of row houses,
Chiren wid yampy in dey eye,
Hearing crowing cocks,
Lil ones jus' wakin' up toh
a day of guesswok,
An' hope,
Days ingrained in me,
Of coal pots and dum' bread
Wid "tin nin" toh give it taste,
Of "badin" pan an'
"pochie" and energetic fowls
runnin' wild, oblivious of
the fact that the next day
they would serve as meal for
the poor children of the yard
Of wooden house of love,

With residents,
assertive women,
Molding and guiding me
And certifying me as a
Legitimate child of Savan,
Branding me forever as
"Savan Yard Chile!"

Culture Defined/Undefined

West Indian culture,
Sacred,
Revered,
minds harking back to more
innocent times,
West Indian culture honored,
Virgin Islands culture
on a pedestal,
culture of ideals,
ideal culture
preserved in iron clad
treasure chests of the mind,
well-conserved in the deepest
enclaves of the heart,
whose clogged arteries testify
to years of neglect,
Sacred Virgin Islands culture
loses some luster when
recast as culprit,
West Indian culture,
Virgin Islands Culture
RECONSTITUTED
viewed from
the perspective of a poor
island nation struggling to survive
in a market not always so
kind,
the struggle for survival
forging overlapping and interlocking

embraces,
Culture seeping through the cracks of
impoverished houses,
Virgin Islands culture preserved on
far-away shelves,
glanced at by all of us
ignoring its natural trait of
intersection with poverty's
sickening path

Labor Of Love*

(*in a souvenir store for tourists, Haiti, 1974; men and boys "*dressed*" only in their underwear, "*working*" in the steamy basement of the store—creating the expensive, profitable artwork sold in that store)

Surprised eyes watching me, looking for solace,
Eyes briefly taking a break from the obscure dungeon,
Place of work for men, boys, scantily clad,
Underwear only, the signature of captivity here

Haitian boys, men, looking upward from their workplace,
Of dejection, of shame, where men dehumanized
By others create for their victimizers treasures of art,
Haitian men, boys carving out the unique statuettes of wood

Stores in the city boast their artwork for tourists like me,
Who seek that which speaks to me of the country's spirit,
Woodwork carved by the souls of men, of boys
Outfitted in underwear in their dungeon of isolation

Sad eyes spying me, and for them I have no answer
As I watch helplessly as other tourists pass by,
Oblivious of the spectacle, the show from the depths of hell,
Boys, men, minimum wage not an issue here in this lost world

Wide eyes beckoning me to hear, or to feel the unspoken words
Of horror, unable to emanate from the mouths of prisoners,
Imprisoned to work, to create their wooden masterpieces,
For suspecting or unsuspecting tourists, like me, marginalizing their existence

Eyes of pain, looking directly at me, tongues unable to utter
Basic truths imprinted in the meager surroundings of the dungeon,
Heavy-laden tongues, paralyzed by fear, by history, by reality,
Unable to muster up the strength to cry, *"Brother, sister, help me!"*

Meanwhile owners of the stores of victimization, of the artistic men and boys,
Chat with tourists like me, who close our eyes so as not to see the
More forceful, piercing eyes, looking downward as they look up from the dungeons,
Where light has no chance of challenging darkness' claim of domination

Haitian eyes, watching me, and begging, and pleading with me to watch also,
So that I might sense within the dungeon of grown men, and boys with no future,
A feeling of desperation, of frustration, and knowing too well the disparity
Of the arrangement, of dreams shattered or deferred, maybe, just maybe forever

Men, boys, whose skillful hands created those monuments of commercial art,
Praised by the onlookers seeking bargains in the stores of exploitation,
Onlookers who refuse to see the trap door at the far side of the store, where hope ends
And the dungeon begins, with its celebrities sophisticatedly clad in their white briefs

Dem Housin' Woman

(for Dr. Sidney Rabsatt)

Dey use' toh call yoh name in dey
Own special way:
"you fo' Miss Maggie,"
"you fo' Miss Beulah"
"you fo' Miss Nita"
"you fo' Emma, come heh"
"you fo' Miss Telma"
"you fo' Miss Eulie"
"you fo' Miss Fina"
"you fo' Miss Eloise"
"you fo' Miss Lily"
"you fo' Miss B"
"you fo' Miss Becca"
"you fo 'Miss Lopie"
go toh La Lechenera,
please buy me a
poun' ah
rice
peas
half poun' ah lard,
you fo' Miss Lee,
come heh,
an' Miss Chrisie own too,
yoh cookin'soup, Ms Jennie?
yes son,
wa' kind ah soup,
Ms Melda?
Black eye peas, son,

save some fo' we,
Miss Sasa food, so good,
smell deh garlic,
reben' Housin' boys,
Frako, and Blackie, Butty, Teddy,
Diamon, Hector, Ponto, Myie
Tony "Maltin," Wayne and Crimmo
dem,
all
coopin' food,
Tito, Dacka,
two most popular boys around deh
Housin' bench wen Miss Sasa cooked her
arroz con pollo y habichuelas,
women, offering guidance to young
lads, needing and seeking it,
dem woman from Housin'
wise, strong, independent,
knowledgeable,
Dem Housin' woman,
so astute, showing you the way,
disciplining you, sharp and swift:
you fo' Maggie, come heh,
yes marm,
get in yoh mudda house, right now,
But…she ain home
No 'but' boy, get in deh house now,
befo' Ah give yoh some…
Yes, licks
from dem
Housin' woman
who
commanded respect,
demanded respect,
earned, and deserved
respect,

from their young charges,
daughters, sons, we were to all,
mothers dey were toh all,
Dem Housin' woman,
Dem woman from Housin'
setting the pace,
being models for
dem Housin' guirls and
deh boys dem too,
dem Housin' woman
spreading themes of
protection
guidance
solidarity
surrogate motherhood,
subscribing to the maxim
<it takes a village>
yea, meson, what women they were!
Dem women from Housin',
dem Pearson Gardens women,
spreading and
preaching the theme of
LOVE!

Yard Child
(Edwin Davis)

Yard filled with sounds of innocence,
Children confirming their faith
In grown-ups,
Agent of their care,
While Sister Esther
Sang her songs of praise
And narrated stories of the Bible's
Smallest adult,
In my Savan Yard of hens and dogs,
And heroines
And little ones like me
Frolicking non stop
Under the Caribbean sun and enduring
The regular gale winds deemed
As friends of the happy children of
The Yard
Playing around wells, on top of wells
Ignoring dangers in our yard of peace
Paying little attention to the outhouses
Stately poised in the most
Unstately ways
Playing in our place of harmony
And joy in my Savan Yard
Of my West Indies
My Savan Yard
Performing its disappearing act
Has only left vague remnants in
Abandoned walls and vestiges

Of unstable shacks marking time
And sacredly guarding narratives
Of yesteryear
Profound memoirs of tiny occupants in
A small space so vast

Look Out Deh Window

(James "Jaime Benítez" Hedringtom)

Fights in the fifties, before, and even several years after
Produced some anger, but more humor and much laughter
Like when mey partna' Jaime panicked from Mimie roun' de fiel'
or wen in secon' grade dis guirl bus mey a cuff, mey head start' toh reel

Combatants used mainly their fists to settle any pending score,
Often the pugilists after one fight vowed to fight maybe once more,
Group of boys or girls, together always in one big bunch
Sometimes after school, or a fight was scheduled after lunch

The entourages represented the seconds or backers of an opponent,
But in general no one besides the fighters even got involved in it
No sah, no street gangs an' dem so comin' lookin' fo' yoh nex' day
No knife, oozies, MK 47, Tech 9, or drive-bys toh make yoh pay

Eyes half shut from some good licks, and ripped-up clothes,
But no evidence of stab wounds jus' some ole good fashion blows
Jus' ah lil' bruise lip, bonkonko, ah not so deep chap in yoh head,
But no wakes, no funerals toh prepare for, 'cause nobardy dead

yoh probably had mo' worry 'bout yoh mudda' who done geh deh news
bu' how yoh wuz rootin' up in deh dut, messin up yoh nice school
shoes,
plus yoh wid yoh chat dat notin' ain gon happen toh yoh wen yoh geh
home,
but yet yoh keep askin' some friens' toh walk wid yoh—scared toh go
alone

nex' day look out deh window, carn' believe wa Ah see, atarl
wa' tis dis! Deh two "*enemies*" out deh jumpin' on deh wall,
frolickin', runnin', tarkin', even on deh same team playin' ball
an' look, one ah dem even now walkin' toh deh odda' one house an' arl!

Identity Shift

Taphus'* name changed,
Identity theft
a 21st century concern,
already perfected in yesteryear by
the guardians of the
West India Company,
Taphus' name changed,
They did not even consult me,
Name changers so busy
Monitoring cargo,
Ships of humanity,
Forgot to call me,
Too many brass chains
to keep bristling in the heat of the
West Indian sun,
Slack ankle bracelets in need of constant
adjustment,
Taphus' name changed in the still and quiet
of the night,
No one called me,
Too many boxes to unload
Too many lives lost
women, children, men
Too many life-less babies
in the deep of the ocean
where the Atlantic flirts with
the Caribbean sea in full
public view,
Taphus had a name change and

could not inform me,
A change completed long before
the restless souls in St. John
Responded against their fate,
Just a normal quest for freedom,
No one bothered to consult them either,
Taphus took a stroll one evening
and on his return
was transformed,
And the King and Queen of Denmark
simply ignored me

*In the 17th century Charlotte Amalia was originally called Taphus by the Danes.

Garn Slingarin'

Reach in deh house,
foot bleedin' an' ting
geh cut from Kasha,
sting-ah-nettle an so'
Mudda' at deh do'
Waitin' fo' yoh

Yoh lookin' sympaty
partna' but dat ain' gon do,
"Mey foot cut up, mammy,
two darg bite meh an' ting,
Plus Kasha and ketch n'keep
hol' on toh meh today"

Yoh mudda don vex, jus' cuttin' yoh eye,
Yoh don frighten, don ready toh bus ah cry,
"Wa' happen, mammy, yoh no longa' like me?
Ah mash' up bad, please mammy, jus' look an' see"

"Way pah yoh went boy? Dat's wat
I *want toh know,*
Now comin' in dis house, no manners in yoh mout',
ackin' like ah pappy sho'

Way Ah sen' yoh, Sonny,
Way Ah sen tell yoh toh go?"
"Toh Miss Annesta, Mammy,
Toh geh some Johnny cake an' so"

"But Miss Annesta don close up lil boy,
so, tell meh way pa' yoh now comin' from?"
"Mammy, honestly, Nantern Joe stap' me,
tell me bu' how Ah mus' go buy he lil rum"

"Bu' afta yoh buy deh ting fo' he
Way pah' yoh went, meson?"
"By Catholic Chuch, Mammy, toh make ah confession,"
"Bu' mey foot hu'tin' from deh darg dem an' deh Kasha,
Ay ya yai, Mammy, toh you none ah dis atarl ain matta'?"

"Come heh toh meh boy
An' bring wid yoh dat big, broad belt on deh chair,
Ah gon wail yoh' tail, cause it look like yoh doan care"
"But Mammy, mey foot don' 'hutin', mey back, and mey han',"
"Well Dat's yoh problem, boy, fo' tryin toh play man,"

Ah wanted mammy to see mey so'(re) foot, feel like Ah lose mey leg,
Yoh see, Ah wuz fearin' ha' blows, so deh mos' Ah cou' do wuz beg
Secko, deh kasha bush and deh mangy darg dem dat ha' don bite me
Coun' match deh pain comin' from dem blows from my MAMMY!

Past Revisited

Rat infested dwellings,
spider webs,
offspring caught within them gleefully,
while gutters with untouchable
disease-bent refuse
sit for endless hours,
impassionate guts of time,
children of the dwellers of the
rat invaded housing play
gleefully too, much like the
innocent offspring in the web
of the spider,
hunger pangs
mediated by sugar and water,
coming together as one,
to perform a good deed
Retrospective glances of yesterday
Highlight moments of glee, of joy,
of wet eyes!
Retrospection idealizes time,
romanticizes moments of history,
of "dry bread" days,
brown suga' and wata',
wata' and suga',
of latrines staring at your door
No signs reading:
"Unhealthy for humans—Don't enter!"
No sign ever spelt
U-N-S-A-F-E!

Glances of retrospection mythicize
the other reality,
the bigger
more overwhelming reality
of Virgin Islands life,
a life known by many, but held in secret,
children of the dwellers of the houses in row,
sworn to secrecy
like the *ñáñigos** of Cuba
guarding sacredly their *Yoruba* selves,
The yard people obliterate through
retrospection
harsh truths,
unpalatable realities,
hiding their diaries from the curious,
and constructing alternate ones,
used exclusively to redefine culture
through the corrosive lens of
P-O-V-E-R-T-Y
*[*ñáñigos* of Cuba, members of the Yoruba Secret Society]

Wey Yoh Sen Meh, Nevis?
(St. Clair Wilkinson)

Nevis look' meh right in mey eye
An' suck he teet,
Complainin' how he ain know meh,
He ain know notin' bout meh,
How Ah tellin' untrut,
Wen Ah tell 'im 'bout mey Granny,
Mary Moving
from Gingerlan'
'bout mey Auntie an' uncle dem,
Nevis bus meh, *"Dem is Crucians,"*
Ah try tellin' Nevis 'bout Ancestry.com,
Nevis laugh' out loud, *"try St Kitts,"*
But St. Kitts sen' meh back toh Nevis
Searchin' fo' Uncle Willy Carroll dem,
In Gingerlan' dey sen' me toh
Charlestown the birthplace of
Alexander Hamilton
Also claimed by St. Croix,
Jus' like mey Granny an' dem,
Crucians tru an' tru like Hamilton,
The Nevisian-Crucian,
Crucian-Nevisian in the
Minds of Crucians,
Virgin Islands' version
Of history,
Nevis, St. Croix claiming this
Founding Father of
Independent America,

Nevis, just like you claim Hamilton
I ask you to claim mey Granny
an dem, mey Nevisian clan,
and in the process, Nevis ancestral home,
mark me and the descendants of
Granny, Mary Moving Burrow,
as yours,
This matriarch and hers emanating
from the bosom
Of Gingerland itself,
Holding the codes
For my
IDENTITY!

POR FIN*

Pues, me esperabas con paciencia
¡Qué sorpresa que nadie me lo dijera!
Pero todo el mundo sabía que yo vendría,
No había secretos en los pueblos
Que algún día te viera yo,
Cuba
Isla de esperanzas y sueños rotos
Una nación con espíritu y ánimo
Me esperabas,
Cuba,
Para informarme de tu gente
Y de que yo pertenezco acá,
Isleño, caribeño, antillano
Que soy yo,
Esperaste mucho tiempo y me
Saludaste
Pero no te hice caso,
Ahora aquí estoy en
Tu corazón
Viendo a La Habana
Sintiendo a La Habana
Conspirando para ser parte
De ti,
Tan feliz soy, Cuba,
Que me hayas esperado,
Ahora reconozco tu sinceridad
Con tus últimas llamadas
Las llamadas animadas

Que me unieron a ti
De una manera que ni aún tus
Más renombrados filósofos y psicólogos
Pueden explicarlo
(*Translation follows)

===

Finally

So you were waiting patiently for me,
What a surprise that no one told me!
But everyone knew that I would come
No secret in the towns
Not in all the pueblos
That I would someday see you
Cuba
Island of broken dreams and hope
Nation of people with spirit, with zest
You were waiting for me
Cuba
To inform me about your people
To inform me that I belong
Islander, Caribbean man, West Indian
That I am
You waited a long time and waved to me
Along the way
But I did not heed your beckoning
So, Cuba, now here I am in the heart
Of your being
Seeing Havana, feeling Havana
Conspiring to be a part of you,
Cuba, so joyous I am that you waited
And now I know than you were sincere
In your final calls, the spirited calls
That connected me to you
In ways that not even your most
Renowned philosophers and psychologists
Can comprehend!

Rock Of Ages

Waves following their own dictates ricochet off rocks
Idly reposed in an isolated corner of the lonely bay,
They stand alone, at times unnoticed,
The ageless island rocks
Refusing to shrink

Stoic, stern in the face of
Persistent waves
Slapping them by the second,
The insults and arrogance of the
Bay's waves
Know no end

And the waves themselves
set no limits of
disruption
discordance
disdain

But the rocks steadily stand
As perennial oppositional gestures that
highlight humanity's fleeting moments

Meanwhile the relentless Caribbean waves beat
in disdainful cacophony against timeless island rocks
That refuse to succumb to erosion's beckoning call

I Weep For You St John
(Kim Lyons)

Tears, first of joy springing
from within,
inside this soul
connected through ancestry,
history and life's
partially recorded truths
to this island's glorious
past
of rebellion
revolution
resistance,
and imprints of blood
and footsteps carved
forever in my island's soil,
and at the foot of precipitous
cliffs the smell of flesh,
symbol of freedom fighters
who chose death over
oppression
over servitude
over enslavement,
tears of joy knowing my DNA
can be traced to that day in
1733,
yet tears of sadness
of grief
viewing you in the distance,
island home,

St. John,
Weep for you I must,
mountain range defamed
defrauded
in the name of progress,
of capitalism's unrelenting
symbolism,
relentless chains of concrete defiling
resting places thought sacred,
acts of heresy
with its acrimonious tone,
I weep for you St John
as you lean lopsided from

the weight of injustice,
of abuse

I see you in the distance
tilting awkwardly,
I weep for you as
residents seek refuge
elsewhere,
chased away by
long held policies marginalizing
them,
the Rockefeller experiment
gone bad,
I spill tears seen by no one,
falling fruitlessly in the
seas and merging with
the same waters that
set the stage for
that fateful day when
Ghanians-Virgin Islanders
cried
ENOUGH

ESENCIA CUBANA

Traté de construirte en la mente
Oh país de misterio
Y una profunda historia,
De tantos compitiendo por supremacía
Durante la época colonial,
Cuba,
No hay ningún novelista,
No hay artista
Ni sociólogo
Que puedan captar tu
esencia
que puedan asegurar que
entiendan las intersecciones
de tus culturas, tradiciones, y creencias
las contradicciones
las paradojas
la compleja idea de
Raza
africanidad
cubanidad
la esencia isleña
la caribeña,
Me desperté
pensando en cómo
crearte
Pero fracasé

Inundado y abrumado
Por realidades que se intersectan y que

¡Me dejan
jadeante!
(***Translation follows**)

==

Cuban Essence

I tried to create you in my mind
Country of mystery
Intense history
Of many vying for supremacy
During the colonial epoch,
Cuba
No novelist, no artist
No sociologist
Can capture your essence
Can claim to understand
The intersections of
Cultures, traditions, beliefs
The contradictions
The paradoxes
The complex idea of
Race
Africanness
Cubanness
Islandness
Caribbeaness,
I awoke devising a plan
To create you
But failed
Inundated and overwhelmed
By intersecting realities
That leave me
Gasping for air!

Carribbean Fusion

West Indian chain connected,
A series of indispensable links,
Las Antillas, we say in Spanish
Diverging and converging visions
Of our geographical and cultural landscape
Islands, some mere dots even on the local map,
Almost nonexistent on national and international
Cartography
Others, like you
Cuba,
Vast unparalleled terrain and
Global relevance,
All islands of our Caribbean archipelago
Joined together by
History's circuitous route

Savanero Haven

African Savan Yard,
Traits of you still seen,
But oh so faintly!
And a tear falls from my eyes
Because you harbor in your
Bosom so many characters,
Of Virgin Islanders,
Of myths and legends
Fused together by time's
Tricky hand,
Melted into our complex history
Of our Danish West Indies
And elaborators of Dutch Creole
Lost in time's cruel linguistic hoax,
My Savan Yard left its faint, barely audible
Ghost-like noises,
Sounds strangely engraved in a few
Wooden partitions
Still standing in defiance of irrelevancy,
Yet loud and pronounced echoes
Resounding in my head
Principal proof of my being
Still a Savanero
While simultaneously laying stakes
In my *Housin'* ground
Which in no way obliterates

Deeply held dreams, memories
Encased forever
Beyond the horizons
Marking eternity

Lasting Bond (Conroy Warren)

Virgin Islands
West Indian
Caribbean
Unbreakable links,
Bonds of sameness,
Likeness
Intersections of cultural tapestries
Customs
Traditions
Blueprints of historical legacies
Priceless culture
Infinite value
Nexus of overlapping identities
Springing from time generated narratives
Of connections
Ancestral trees with marked branches
Denoting generational linkage to
Entrenched roots firmly positioned
In the bosom of our shared realities
Rich culture inseparable from
The value of life,
Understood only when seen through
The lens of history told
Then retold through a constant
Process of recalibration,
Caribbean
West Indian

but meantime
some nice sug'an water,
dry bread an' arl will do
No shame admittin'
none ah dis ah tarl!!!

========================*Cuba*========================

REFLEXION

Escribir sobre ti, Cuba,
Es imaginarte en tu larga historia,
Ecos de gritos de seres humanos
Transportados a tus orillas
Sin ninguna consideración
Por las almas destruidas en un avalanche
De decisiones amargas,
Ambiciones codiciosas, avariciosas,
Ver tu tierra expansiva
Es ceder a emociones multiples
Sobre la opresión en siglos pasados
Sobre la explotación y subjugación
Por los poderosos en aquel entonces,
Versificar sobre ti, isla contradictoria,
Es sentir el espíritu
De un alma que se ha despertado
Viéndose a sí misma en un
Reflejo de los rayos de esperanza
Producidos por un brilliante
Sol antillano
(***Translation follows**)

==

Reflection (Myron Jackson)

To write about you, Cuba
Is to imagine you in your long history
Echoes of screaming beings
Transported to your shores,
Without any consideration
For the souls destroyed in an avalanche
Of bitter decisions,
Greedy and avaricious ambitions,
Seeing your expansive land
Is to yield to multiple emotions
About oppression in past centuries
About exploitation and subjugation
By the powerful during that time,
To create verses about you, contradictory island,
Is to feel the spirit
Of a soul that has now awaken
Seeing itself in the reflection
Of the rays of hope,
Produced by a brilliant West Indies sun

Big Gut

The big gutter reposes idly
next to the row of houses,
wooden structures
connected by dreams,
by hope,
by poverty's swift and sure hand,
hand of fate signaling destiny's
ways

the quiet gut at times
vaguely rumbles as it
transports its cargo,
its litany of life signs adjacent to the houses,
disconnected and
fragmented by hierarchal systems of power,
the undercurrent that propels the gut
with its treasures discarded there long ago

the gut
secretly records voluminous data that speak
truths of the dwellers
of the houses in row
inseparably joined by uneven doctrines
and strategies
designed to construct Virgin Islands identity,

The construction process persists as the contents
of the big gut gush by
ignoring the passers-by traversing it,
who in turn ignore the gutter
and its unique skill at
status identification

Awkward Move
(Dr. Simon B. Jones-Hendrickson)

Moving sideways,
islands jostle each other,
Intersecting pasts,
reconfiguration
upheavals in the underbellies of shifting
gliding
feinting
sliding cultures

West Indies, island nations,
shielding themselves from
themselves
repositioning mirrors of reflection,
opting for broken splinters of glass,
broken glasses,
pieces strewn about,
images barely seen

Contorted reflection
Unintegrated islands, at their
maximum state of decomposition,
disfigurement
splintering of splinters
Fractured mirrors of multiple images
Decompartmentalized images,
awkward glimpses of one another,
from the perspective of jagged edges

Looking askance the islands appear
inverted and uneven,
Fractionalization completed
They seem to be moving,
predictably, obliquely,
SIDEWAYS

Ah Gon Flit Yoh
(Shirlene Williams Lee)

Ah hea' yoh is ah lil pesky ting wid ah pretty wing
Admirable some say, yoh duz hum nice an' even sing
Buzzin in people ear wid dat jarrin' monotonous tone
Yoh drivin' us crazy, fella, we want toh be left alone

I have toh have ah short chat wid you, mey annoyin' frien'
Yoh see, yoh makin' us mad; dat funny-up noise mus' en'
Because of yoh hummin' an' buzzin' nobardy even carn sleep
Wen yoh cum attackin' people, deh fear we have ah yoh is deep

Ah hea' how yoh bring some virus from some strange place way out yanda,
Everbardy now complainin' about dis mean frien ah yours, Chikungunya
Take yoh ole disease back wid yoh, geh it outta heh we beg yoh please
We doan welcome it at tarl no place down here in our West Indies

We don tired of all yoh carryin' on wid yoh stuippidness
Get goin,' move out pesky one, jus' go 'bout yoh business
Yoh is deh cause ah pain in people han', leg, deh knee dem an' so
Believe me, untame' insect, all mey neighbors dem don disgus' ah yoh

Ah feel like callin' dem ole V.I. smoke truck fo' yoh flimsy, disgustin' self
Yoh ain' geh no shame, why not hang out in deh carnar of some dutty shelf?
Instead of pollutin' deh air wid dat buzzin' soun' dat nobardy like toh hear,
But yoh keep doin' it, so we know, troublesome one, dat yoh really ain care

Yoh lucky, dem smoke truck days don, neva' toh return again
Wen we use' toh dance behin' deh truck celebratin' yoh pain,

But every year it look like yoh jus'keep gehin' stronga' an' stronga'
Accordin' toh wa' deh people dem say yoh mutate into ah insect monsta'

Yoh maybe look weak, but deh Hulk ain geh notin' atarl ova' you,
Deh people dem want toh trow up deh hans', dey ain know wa toh do
Yoh maybe tink' it's cute toh cause ah lot ah pain arl ova people body,
But lisen heh, Mr. Troublemaker, makin' people miserable ain' funny

Baygon and Insecticide look like dey doan trouble yoh no mo'
Dat's why yoh now so conceited an' will not jus' leave an' go
But Ah have ah secret weapon, Ah warnin' yoh, givin' yoh time toh run
'Cause after many years Ah still have mey mudda' ole reliable *flit gun*!

ASCENDENCIA

Abuelo se fue y tuvo mucho éxito
Cortando caña y ayudando a sostener
La economía dominicana
Pero también vino acá,
Cuba,
A tus orillas
Para trabajar en los *cañaverales*,
Acá en tu tierra veo rostros
De gente que señala que me conoce
Pues son descendientes de los dedicados cortadores
De caña
Quienes recorrieron nuestras Antillas,
Un día en La *Habana Vieja*
oí una voz,
Examiné uno de los rostros
Lo cual confirmó mi sospecha
(*Translation follows)

==

Ancestry (Dr. Ronald "Husky" Harrigan)

Grandfather left and excelled at his job
Cutting cane and helping to sustain
La Dominicana economy
But also came here,
Cuba,
To your shores
To work the canefields, the *cañaverales*,
Here in your land I see faces,
Of people signaling without words that they know me
Because they are descendants of the dedicated cutters
Who traversed our *Antillas*, our West Indies,
One day in La *Habana Vieja*
I heard a voice,
And examined one of the faces,
Confirming my suspicion

Nación Unica

País complicado
Nación compleja
Mi isla vecina, esta Cuba
En Holguín, Matanzas, La Habana Vieja
Se ven varias imágenes
De esta región caribeña
Patria de Lima, Morejón
Pedroso, Guillén
Dentro de ella diversidad cultural sin fin
Una bella física, pero aún más del alma
Llegué a sus orillas tratando de entenderla
Con la meta de acercarme más a mi isla hermana
(*Translation follows)
===

Unique Nation

Complicated country
Complex nation
My neighboring island, this Cuba
In Holguín, Matanzas, La Habana Vieja
Various images of this Caribbean nation
Lima's, Morejón, and Guillén's
Country
Cultural diversity without end
A physical beauty, but more so of the soul
I came to her shores trying to understand her
With the goal of getting closer to my sister island

In This Space

(To my St. Croix family, Glen Byron, Deanna Sackey)

Deep inside of me,
lies a place, quietly
positioned in the deepest enclaves
of my Identity,
self-labeling,
a place, that also named
me in language so symbolic
no one need ask my name,
this place that quietly
reposes within me has
too, quietly,
told me who I am,
a reality guarded safely,
within me
The place within me
calls not itself
"Place,"
calls itself no name,
but I know it by name,
though it seeks no credit for
shaping me
defining me,
but knows it has,
this place, has molded me
and those
linked to me
by **DNA AND**
Links of spirit and soul,

This place, site of the long
arduous journey of
granny Burrow,
This place,
St. Croix, Santa Cruz
Ay Ay,
home place of those
        in Grove
        La Vallee
        Frederiksted,
        Christiansted,
        Gingerland
        of those forever linked to me

Stroll On Sacred Soil

no protest by present inhabitants
on the soil,
vague knowledge of time past,
of lost villages reconfigured below
by default in time own terms,
no protest from below where
conversion long ago took place,
of bones to ashes
of hearts to soul,
dreams long ago transformed into
nightmarish scenes of stark reality,
residents behind their gates of
detachment
defacing daily the sacred ground,
below hiding past residences
in the bosom of the earth,
converted to hell,
preserving souls of the countless
whose lives spelt martyrdom,
strolling in the streets in my neighborhood
my thoughts remain transfixed,
the earth palpitates beneath my feet
and with each throb sends reminders of
West Indian narratives,
words recounting yesteryears'
wicked prisons
of dehumanization,
suppression,
Between the earthly palpitation,

I feel a force pushing against the
sole of my feet,
the force of
those trapped,
forgotten beneath
the Virgin Islands' concrete structures
silenced again by
the power of amnesia
and of distortion,
and
time's final death knell:
its blow of
oblivion

Two Lickings
(Fo' dem Housin' Boys)

They used toh lick our hair,
den lick us wid dey belt,
dem blows ah hut,
our mudda dem,
fo' swimmin' on deh bayside, o
boathouse,
without permission,
Savan boys dem went deh boathouse,
Bull an' dem,
dem Housin' boy went Pantoom,
Tito, Jarmon and Diggy,
Reovan and Elrod dem,
Round Deh Fiel' boys
use' toh swim
wayever dey could get ah
dip in deh ocean blue,
Boisie, Tatun, Skippy dem

Deh best swimmers,
Dem Bayside boys jump off deh jarring rocks
right down de on deh bayside,
with its wide
unobstructed view of the ocean vast
symbolizing dreams of little
West Indian children

but our mudda dem
used toh beat

wid hard belt,
"Yoh went toh swim today, meyboy?"
No mammy, no
"Pappa God gon punish yoh, son"
"No, mammy, no,"
Docka an' dem went,
Fordy an Myie dem,
Wayne an'dem,
Bayie Sela an' Bayie Fish Eye,
Dem boys from "down-ah-side" went,
Like Snakin,' Clarka, an' 88, Touchie and he brodda Buddy,
Husky an Scala, Lip, an' Magoo dem
Sidney dem went
and Tino Colón,
an' he brudda, Hook Shot Colón,
not me,
Out comes the TONGUE,
exploring mey hair dat dem call nappy,
den deh BELT,
arl deh neighbor dem know
dat tis time for her
to shed blows,
Ms Chrisie, Ms Beulah,
Ms Becca, Ms Eloise,
wuz sheddin' blows too,
next day Bayside
an' deh Savan boy dem
tell of their own episodes,
Ah tell yoh,
Dem mudda
tongue geh magic
yoh hea'!

Kingship
(Tregenza Roach)

Ghanaians stare at me and
I at them
We share *DNA*
Looking in their eyes
I see genetic makeup linked
To granny
The Nevisian woman who claimed St. Croix,
I stare at Ghanaians and they stare back,
We both smile,
Refusing to boast of a truth
But proud to guard it
In the indecipherable parts of our souls

I speak "Ghanaian"
Or maybe "Nigerian"
I speak African, a language not uttered,
But linguistically referenced in our gazes,
In search of the link, not seen but known,
Not seen, not known, but reassured,
The paradox of the *DNA* riddle,
Unsolved and irresolvable,
But not at all complex,
I stare in the mirror,
And see Africa,
Then Ghana, then Nigeria, claimed me,
Kenya called me its own,
Africa then claimed me,
And I was afraid to claim Africa

But in a moment of assurance
Africa whispered: *"My child,"*
a sound still reverberating in my head,
a sound of praise to Africa,
and a salute to the discoverer of
DNA, who promised me that I can be decoded,
After the words of comfort I returned to claim
Africa
But the Ghanaian and Nigerian in me
Refused to be unrecognized,
And said they will not remain unclaimed,
I stared at Ghana who declared:
"I know you; you belong to me,"
I then claimed all of Africa,
Ghana smiled its approval

Caribbean Mash-Up

Meh Caribbean mash-up,
What ah ting!
Roofs flying all about
Concrete collapsing,
Domino effect,
Irma and her band of gangsters,
José an' dem so,
María with her bad attitude,
Adding insult to injury,
Cocobay 'pon ton ah yaws!
Pouncin all ova meh Caribbean,
Our archipelago uprooted and upended,
Twisted and turned
"Apocalypse," cried my fellow islanders,
"Deh en' comin'"
While seeking shelter in shelter-less places,
My Caribbean—mess' up an' mash-up,
Houses, cars, debris, floating in deh air,
Streets renamed "RIVERS,"
Sea indistinguishable from road,
Meh Caribbean screamin' foh aid,
Islands lost within the chaos of
mericless winds hammering,
Pounding, bashing, crashing, slashing
Beating,
Mean Irma, soul-less María,
Meh Caribbean mash-up bad meson!
Vegetation altered
A metamorphis marked for eternity,

"ISLANDS GARN" Residents shout in chorus
Flattened by satanic forces,
Unbridled and undisciplined,
Mash-up. Watta mash up!
Our Caribbean mash-up,
Digging out of bitter sadness
And hopelessness,
Meh Caribbean beat down,
Tourists garn,
Threatening to stay away from
Meh Caribbean,
Meh home mash down,
Meh home wash out,
Meh Caribbean mash up!
But with eyes wide opened,
Down but not out,
Our Caribbean promising
To rise again,
Meh Caribbean like the
Relentless phoenix, vying for
Resurrection in a heartless
Process of atmospheric dehumanizatiom
And unspeakable destruction!

Down Under

What's beneath those seas,
forever faithful Virgin Islands waters
Standing the test of eternity?
DNA of past epochs mixes
undetectably, indecipherably
with the water, the salt,
stored secret genes
of potential lost,
of lost possibilities
all wiped away by the overarching
state-sponsored,
government sanctioned
often church supported
plan of aggression
captivity, subjugation,
Whose bones disintegrated in
the deepest enclaves of the mysterious,
geographical wonders of the sea,
Of my Virgin Islands' waters,
Sworn to secrecy, trying to absolve itself
Declaring
NO ORAL REVELATION?
Who lie beneath the ocean next to the
artifacts that were accomplices in
sealing their fate?
Corrupt artifacts
of chains, of shackles
that permitted themselves to be used,
exploitative chains of irons

chains of brass
willing participants of the genocidal acts
And now refusing to cooperate,
refusing to inform,
knowing well the answers to key questions
But declining to participate in
solving history's cross word puzzle,
the riddle of a well-designed evil,
Who lies there next to the jewelry,
chains of time, underworld of silence
underworld boasting of no
deeds of complicity,
in those seas that whisper only faint
unfamiliar sounds?

Island Jockeys
(Elaine Jacobs)

West Indian islands
Still jockeying for position
In a vain game of comparative importance,
Fed constantly by globalization's
Tricky and slick plan,
Islanders squeeze their neighbors, themselves
Vying for first place in the market place
Of false inventions and distorted images,
West Indies islands busy changing themselves,
Busy altering courses and directions,
Our West Indies fighting to please,
Struggling to redefine
Reinvent ourselves to
Earn the dollar spent in our stores
Of vices and toys,
West Indies pushing each other
Out of position to position each itself
As destination NUMERO I in the
Backbiting world of global tourism,
Reaching our shores and clearing
Clean our spaces that were once
Filled with
Pride
Dignity
Sense of identity
Honor
West Indianness,
My West Indian islands fighting

For top billing to be crowned
Island #1,
Best Island
Kind Island
Good natives,
My West Indies fell
For the trap,
And must continue to jockey for
Position
To win the top prize
"Best Native Award"

Darg So Mangy I

Ah mangy dog bite meh back ah mey leg one day
Bu' he leave mey brudda dem alone,
Dem mangy darg have fangs, not teet'
Deh mangy darg bite meh up de by Harbour View
Oh, some decades ago, but dis arl true

He soak' ah bite in mey calf
Bu' Ah didn' really worry
'cause mey mudda had
—bittah bush home
—*macuricome* on deh shelf
—some kind ah lard from up by
REDBALL

Dat crazy mangy darg
pass' by mey brudda' dem
mey sista' dem,
den sink he teet' in meh,
—Ah put *marcuricome*
—Ah put lard
—Ah drink bittah bush
—den some inflammation bush
—lata' pu' lil bay rum on it.
—soak mey foot in Epson Salt

Nex' time Ah see da half-dead darg,
he tongue largin' out
like he fo' *Little Red Ridin'Hood*
Ah gon cut' 'im eye,

he gon know Ah vex
'cause dem mangy darg too conceited

arrogant mangy canine, integral
cultural component of our land,
Deh Mangy Darg of the Virgin Islands

Mangy darg bite meh 'cause he feel that
deh Virgin Islands geh' he on ah
PEDESTAL,
Mangy darg, Ah ain' 'fraid yoh,

Mammy geh enough bittah bush
An' *macuricome*
toh protect me from yoh scaly self

María, Who Sen' Yoh?

María, who sen yoh?
Yoh even ain know wey
Deh Caribbean was befo' dis,
Bu' yoh fin' us,
Tell deh trut', María,
Who sen' yoh?
If it tain Satan, tain deh devil
Not Lucifer,
Who it tis den?
Building fallin' down,
Mud all ova deh place,
People dem carn leave deh
house,
Deh scared,
Mold in deh house,
In deh wok place,
Yoh make meh nephew Dell sick
Wid yoh stuiepiness,
Meh people feelin' stress', feelin' strain'
Because ah deh bad weather,
Because ah you, María,
Ah want toh call yoh Mary,
But ah fraid,
Yoh might feel insulted,
Who it tis sen' yoh
Toh cause all dis distruction,
All dese problems?
María, Mary, wa eva yoh name,
Some people say dey hea' yoh

Comin'
"She roun' deh carna' comin',
Roarin' like ah lion,
Howlin' like ah wolf"
Relax, so people in mey Caribbean cou' relax,
Look wa' yoh do toh Puerto Rico,
No shame in yoh heart,
Not a drop ah tears in yoh eyes
Ah hea' how yoh brag all day an' night,
How nobardy cou match yoh,
How Harvey, Irma, an' José ain notin'
Yoh tell people how yoh was category
6, wen there is no such ting,
Yoh is ah disgrace, María,
Yoh love no one,
Care for none,
Ah ain even sure yoh like yoself
Ah mean, yoh wicked self,
But, who sen' yoh heh?
Confess, tell deh trut fo' once in
Yoh life,
Save yoself, María,
From yoh wicked self
We glad toh see yoh leave,
F I N A L L Y!
Go bout' yoh business,
Back to deh open ocean,
Wey nobardy gon see you,
O' hea' yoh,
O' hea' 'bout yoh,
O' study yoh,
Yoh left yoh imprint on our Caribbean
On our West Indian world
Dat will neva be the same,
And I tink yoh still laughin'
An' snortin',

Still actin disorderly
Pattin yohself on yoh back
For a job well done!!
But untamed one,
Disgustin' ting,
Ah still doan know
WHO SEN YOH MESON?!

PART II

Alarm Clock
(In memory of Dr. Lezmore Emmanuel)

Africa woke me from my sleep,
I was startled,
A long interrupted sleep
Of silence,
Africa stood in a corner and shouted
My name,
In a language I understood
But unintelligible to others,
Africa renamed me,
In a ceremony worthy of praise,
Then shouted out my name and spoke
Volumes to me,
I responded with no conscious
Pre-thought
Africa made my response unconscious
And praised me:
"That is good, my son,"
Africa spoke silently to me,
I looked around,
No one else seemed to know,
No one else seemed to care,
Abject Silence in my Virgin Islands
In my West Indies!
Africa uttered many stories
Known only to the continent,
I was implicated by
Unlocking the stories,
Then humbled,

Africa spoke to me in codes,
"*Dream in Africa,*
Dream dreams of dreamers who
Also dream in Africa,"
Africa was calling me home,
Africa asked me questions
To which I had no response,
Asked me to explain secrets
I never heard about,
Asked me about the Virgin Islands
And Ghana, and Nigeria
About St. John, St. Thomas, St. Croix
I woke from my sleep startled,
And Africa,
Standing tall, proud
With a look of defiance,
Silently encouraged:
"*Be Africa; be me,*"
Once I heard that directive
The knees began to quiver,
I felt the rush of blood in my veins,
My heart began to beat much faster,
Circulating in my head were
endless images of my West Indies
My Virgin Islands,
Africa smiled and signaled for me to relax,
A now calm soul,
Lost in the moment of history,
History's prisoner
Glorious and traumatic,
Africa shouted my name
Then others began to look at two of us,
Others began to hear the echo of the
Booming voice of the Continent,
Africa called other names
Africa then called thousands

Then millions of names,
Echoes were reverberating in the Americas,
In Europe
In Asia
In Australia
Where the children of
The Diaspora were
Responding,
The earth shook in the Virgin Islands
Throughout all the Caribbean,
Africa woke me from a profound sleep,
And I refuse to close my
Eyes again

Coromantees*—St. Johnians Unbent

The Coromantees,
Strong, willful, determined
Ghanians claiming their space,
In a space not theirs,
But laying down their stakes
Rejecting rejection in their new home
Beautiful, St. John
DWI
Home of these Virgin Islanders-Africans
Sifted through the turbulent waters
Of the Atlantic, landing in the Virgins of the
DWI
Rebelling, Refusing, Refuting
REBELLING
All elements of the Crown
Designed to enslave
Dehumanize
Reduce to rubbles of nothing,
To create objects of these Coromantees
Loan to St. John for all time
Restless, dissatisfied souls
Formed, Shaped
By a Formidable Continent
That never forgot them
While far away in the
DWI,
They pushed and shoved
Screamed in protest
Blood stains in Cruz Bay soil,

Still a detectable smell in the air,
Pride of new Virgin Islanders
Shaking off the yoke
Gathering, Planning, Conniving
Failing by choice, By RIGHT
To answer the Masters' calls,
In communicating with each other
Ghana making its mark on
St. John soil,
Their footprints still present
In these islands in the sun,
The Coromantees spoke truth,
A sound that will reverberate
Eternally in the deep valleys of my St. John

*A reference to the Akan group of the Gold Coast (Ghana)

King Of The Diamond
(For Adelbert Hendricks / Morse Hendricks)

He cherished his sport like no one
I had ever known,
Spending hours of self-training
Even done in his home

He knew the ins-and-outs of the game he loved,
Dedicated, committed, as if inspired from above,
As a young boy he already showed evidence of his skills
Guided steadily by a clear vision and an unshakable will

No one else on the island of St. Thomas could match his play
Because he worked with great purpose on his art every day
Batting, running and above all endlessly pitching and catching that ball
This young man knew where he was heading without any doubt at all

No matter the limitations the critics tried to set for this unique player
He worked hard every day, and thus totally discredited every naysayer,
Never arrogant, never selfish, never vain, just dedicated to his chosen art
What an athlete, such a great player, overcoming obstacles from the start,

During an era not many years removed from the legacy of Jackie Robinson
He had to fight against the odds, against segregation, and racism—that
poison
But Elrod "Ellie" Hendricks was not one to be deterred by any obstacle,
Never sat around idly waiting patiently for the appearance of some miracle,

He proved to be a fighter, a man with an inner strength and determination
Fearless, relentless, always approaching his sport with the utmost dedication

Ellie Hendricks truly was very special, the product of the island called "Deh rock,"
He always encouraged all players to become better to fully invest in their sport stocks

Representing his Virgin Islands on both the national and international sphere
Catching, batting, and performing, he was a star whose talents were displayed
Hail to Ellie who never ever distanced himself from his Virgin Islands
No matter his years with the Orioles or Yankees residing on the mainland

He honored his West Indian roots and was a very proud Caribbean man
This iconic figure always respected Virgin Islands culture and traditions,
In these Virgin Islands everyone should forever remember his name,
Even though he never sought any praise, special recognition or fame

For Elrod Hendricks has brought glory to his countless number of baseball fans
While simultaneously honoring his cherished and beloved Caribbean homeland
What an example, quite a model, this extraordinary and gifted sports figure
Indeed he should be enshrined in the hearts of all Virgin Islanders forever!

Certification

Islands passing through the
Sifting time of history
The yo-yo effect of rejection
And acceptance,
Island home with huge manifests,
Names of those laying the base
For our future survival,
Ancestors long forgotten,
Ancestors long discounted,
Discarded as irrelevant

Islands shuffling along history's
Rugged pathways,
Learning to blame ourselves
For present day realities
Always deemed detached
From history's zigzagging course,
Virgin Islanders caught within
A confusing web of accountability
And the body blows dealt by yesterday's
Fisticuffs thrown with malice

West Indies, parrying at times to blunt
The effects of the blows,
Deceive itself, walking aimlessly
In a tunnel with no discerning light at the end,
Islanders overwhelmed by social determinism
Accept our blueprint of fate
In a vicious game of self-hate and blame,

While the designers of history
Smile and laugh
Centuries at a time,
Their mission complete
Then authenticated and certified
by the Islanders ourselves,
Reciprocating smiles of
Ambivalent approval

Self-Reflection
(Edgar Lake)

West Indies overly anxious to divert from
Its past,
A headless creature with no path to follow,
Our West Indies, claiming, only reluctantly,
remote kinship
To that huge continent,
Our West Indies too often afraid of itself,
Sneaking up to the mirror,
Hoping to see a distortion of the original,
West Indies concealing itself
Behind multiple masks,
To obliterate histories' timelines,
Self-reflections have caused
Subtle damages to the eyes,
And now the West Indies blink
While in front of the mirror
Capturing in minute seconds the
Fragments of genealogy
Of lineage,
West Indies closed its eyes,
Subjecting itself to dizzying spells,
Constructing imaginary signs:
*"West Indies, Under Construction,
Stand back."*
Islands seeking exotic connections
Maximize history's extensive data
To rearrange itself
To realign itself:

"West Indies—re-invented!"
The vast AFRICAN Continent
casts its formidable shadow over
tiny West Indies,
and we try to keep our eyes closed
but the West Indies sun,
aware of the trickery at hand,
summons an abundance of light
that forces the eyes to open,
the West Indies will gradually begin
to see
the shadow of the huge continent
and in it
the traits inherited:
strength
resistance
pride
passed down by the resilient Continent,
the West Indies will look
at the shadow cast and
begin the process of connecting dots,
Africa cast its huge shadow
Then sent its message to the new
Generation,
Past and present generations sat
Together
In the shade of the huge shadow
Cast,
With the beaming sun
Bearing witness to a relationship
Promising to be eternal,
Africa smiled many times,

And the West Indies trembled when
It heard in the most assertive and affirmative voice:
"Children of the Diaspora,
look in the mirror of truth
and see me"

Family Values

Vivid visions of slavery stick in my head
of families pulled apart
to jump start a stagnant economy,
to promote a thriving business,
international business,
international relations,
no true relationships,
special jewelry,
bracelets of liberty loss
the clink-clank of the manacles that in
loud silence
announce the blissful matrimony
of bride and broom

Here comes the bride,
the groom
their offspring of doom,
Visions parade in my head
of slavery's pernicious ways
To Brazil
be off,
To Cuba
be gone,
To South Carolina
go you,
To Puerto Rico
Virgin Islands,
St. John, Tortola, St, Thomas
St. Croix, Virgin Gorda,

Visions float uncontrollably in my mind,
Baby to the highest bidder,
No name baby?
Parents more profitable as two,
Less profitable as a couple,
separate, but unequal,
nebulous pension plan
In the well-structured economic
program of avarice,
GREED,
the true WMD of the America's
Self-styled anarchy,
Designated Annihilation of the
nuclear family

See No Evil...

Nations of islands rising from jagged
edge boulders
spring from the seas of yesteryear,
volcanic ashes unevenly
interspersed,
mingling with the soil
of the land,
Nation islands
Island nations
Ocean waves terminating
against the base of
rocks of the Americas,
witnesses of countless acts of
inhumanity

Rocks without eyes
or tongue
yet witnesses of strife,
of mutiny
Clandestine operations,
Rocks with no writing instruments
to record brutalities,
kidnappings,
subversions
betrayals at the highest level

Jagged rocks,
boulders without shoulders,
shouldering no responsibility

for deeds,
unspeakable deeds,
coming to fruition in the seas
wetting the rocks sitting impatiently,
perhaps anxious to somehow tell a
story never before chronicled

Bottomless Socks Of Truth
(For my brother, Eldridge)

Boys, girls, wearing their socks,
socks worn only in prime time,
socks pulled up high,
a tradition, an island custom,
integral part of the ideology
of culture,
Socks worn right,
Set right to conform to traditional
Norms,
Virgin Islands cultural virtues,
evidenced by
the socks stretched to the max
Socks hidden within shoes,
school shoes
church shoes
Shoes of status
securely hiding socks
within them,
Socks worn high,
tradition of
poverty's ways of fabricating,
poverty's manner of hiding
truth
reality,
poverty's trick of
fusion,
of style,
Socks worn high to the top

Socks with no bottom
Socks of those at the bottom,
Socks of the latest style,
high fashioned
socks of poverty,
poverty the trickster,
allowing no one to peek
within the shoes of status,
Socks of the poor,
in their sock adornment,
Socks pulled high depicted
the Virgin Islands
other truth covered artfully
by the shoes of class and status

Ah Ain' Bitin No Finga'*

Look heh, I ain 'fraid ah no Cow Foot Woman, Jumbie, an' ting
Ah cou' pu' mey han' in ah jack spania' nes' and doan geh sting
Mey gran'father was ah obeah man who duz still keep me in sight
Dat's why yoh see Ah duz walk in dem cemetery past midnight

Big man duz run from me wen gran'pa standin' by mey side
dem who duz sic Jumbie 'pon people, wen dey see meh dey duz hide,
deh Jumbie dem deyselves duz keep dey distance from me, yoh know
'tis true that sometimes wen dey see meh dey say: *"Sorry, Ah ga' toh go!"*

One day Ah point toh deh graveyard an' forget toh bite mey finga',
Arl deh neighbors stopped by mey house, warnin': "boy yoh in danja'."
"How much time Ah don tell ah yoh dat finga' bitin' ain fo' me
Only fo' deh people dem who have fear of dem roamin' Jumbie?"

Some jealous ah meh since dey hea' of mey granfadda ties,
Now dey 'fraid toh even look at meh straight in mey eyes
Fo' fear dat Ah gon 'cause someting' strange toh happen toh dem
But deh fact is Ah have no special powers, Ah want dat lie toh en'

"But how come yoh duz walk deh graveyard like yoh doan care?" asked Husky
"Ah don' tell yoh ah million times, Secko, mey Gran'pa duz always protec' me,
Dis good man duz guide an' advise me and make sure dat Ah out of harm's way
Dat's why yoh duz see me walkin' 'roun' like ah bad man on deh islan' eveyday"

"But yoh still need toh bite yoh finga' wen yoh point at dat place," said
some man,
"No," I responded, *"Ah ain goin' toh do nothin' dat could someday damage*
mey han',

103

Spirits, jumbies, arl Ah dem dey scared toh be in the same place wey dey see me standin'
'Cause dey know mey gran'pa quite well, so as dey see meh dey duz take off runnin'!

*As children in the 50's we were suspicious that pointing to a graveyard brought bad luck, which could only be averted by "*bitin' yoh finga.*"

Artificial Bonds
(Dr. Vincent Cooper)

West Indian islands, part-time friends,
know each other, but not too well,
These lands surrounded by seas,
Several islands chatted with each
other one day,
but did not communicate,
But they spoke one day
and left future meetings to chance encounters

Islands hiding from neighbors behind
enormous boulders adding charm to
their beaches
already enchanted by grainy white sand,
Portable alliances and bonds,
Fleeting friendship formed betwixt the
shifting sands of the cays and bays

West Indian islands,
strangers in the night
exchanging glances in the still
of the night
Trying to preserve their own spaces
on soil tracing their heritage to
volcanoes
tsunamis
quakes

West Indian nations looking

at each other in the face but
reluctant to open their eyes,
fearful of recognition,
uncovered relationships
common history
intersecting paths
similar voices howling in the dark,
fearful of deeper acquaintance,
stronger ties,
fearful of seeing eyes that see eyes
seeing them

Nation Of Nobility
(Dr. Alexandra Cornelius)

Haiti will get its chance one day
To bask in the sun of its true glory,
of its unparalleled past
History of rebellion
of revolution
Revolt,
Haiti, noble nation,
Do not fall prey to the
designators of evil,
designers of your
assumed demise,
Haiti will get its chance one day
and will only smile when
her detractors see her rising from
ashes, Caribbean Phoenix

Haiti will smile,
then laugh,
Finally placed where it
rightfully belongs
–model nation
–nation of resistance
of grandeur,
Haiti will have its day
and observers will ask themselves
who allowed this to happen?
Who permitted the disparagement
–exploitation

–repression?

Haiti, your response,
your reaction will reveal in
no uncertain terms the
TRUTH—
that without you
our West Indies would have
one less shining example
of inner strength,
fortitude

That model for insatiable quest for freedom!

Royal Christening

Taphus* screamed at the news,
his strong voice heard in
the steep hills and deep valleys,
in the enclaves of the majestic
seas of the Caribbean
and the Atlantic

Clandestine collusion,
Kings, Queens
and other cohorts in Europe
sending the news,
Taphus and the slaves trembled
Upon hearing the news of
Taphus' identity transplanted,
The King's wish,
Enough to inspire change,
Taphus confused
gracefully accepted
his new identity

Inhabitants of Taphus sang songs,
Songs of the new baptism,
riveting tunes
reverberating in the far reaches of
Christiansted, Frederiksted
La Vallee, Road Town

Taphus turned his back
but for a second, and the namers

of the *Gades* performed tricks of magic,
Magical denominational shifts,
Taphus coughed and momentarily closed
his eyes,
Already blinded by bitter circumstances,
But eyes not too blind to see the scars on the skin,
ears hearing lashes in the night,
under the moonlight
"Moonlight shining bright tonight" sang the
inhabitants of Taphus

Taphus rested from the acts of a vicious night
and awoke to hear a new song,
being sung on a day recorded
For eternity when the
King and Queen bequeathed a new
identity on a night
of stunning baptism

*In the 17th century Charlotte Amalie was originally called Taphus by the Danes.

CUBAFRICA

Qusiera definirte,
Cuba, si me lo permitieras,
Eres el Continente en América
Transformada por el proceso
De <transculturación>
Pero andando en América
Bien vestida del gran Continente,
Te pido una oportunidad de
Categorizarte, nación antillana,
Con la promesa de hacerlo
Con pocas palabras,
O con una sola,
Decir que eres tú,
Sin duda,
Cuba,
<Africa>

===

Cubafrica

I would like to define you,
Cuba, if you would allow me,
You are the Continent in Latin America
Transformed through the process
Of <transculturation>
But walking in Latin America
Dressed up in Africaness
I beg you for the opportunity
To categorize you, West Indian nation,
With the promise that I will do so
in a few words,
or in one word only,
And say that you are
Undoubtedly,
Cuba,
<Africa>

Santa Cruz/Cuba

Matanzas, Cuba to Calimete
West End, St. Croix to East End
Moments of history that we choose to forget
Cultural patrimony deeply
And richly hinged to my
St. Croix,
Santa Cruz,
I see reflections of you in the
Magnificent landscape of
A place
Much more expansive,
in the bosom of Cuba,
this island nation,
Yet telling similar stories
Through the unseen ashes
Diffused below our extensive canefields
Concealing painful
narratives

Mommy Heh Now

He larng' out he tongue at deh neighbor, Miss Mavis,
Den suck he teet,
He frien' dem encourage him "Partna', dat's so cute, so neat"

Wus' yet, he started cussin' bad word an' cuttin' he eye
"Yoh been very rude young fella," said Miss Mavis
Ah warnin' yoh Lil' boy, Ah jus' ain gon put up wid dis"

"Mey mudda ain' home and Ah cou' do wa Ah want
Ah don' cuss Mr. Willy an' Tam deh driver of deh ole truck"
"Well, well, boy, keep it up, yoh gon soon run outta luck

'Cause somebardy gon give yoh ah bonkonko
Dey gon bump up yoh eye, wait, yoh gon see
keep up yoh rudeness, lil fella
Dat person, might jus' be me."

"Well, mommy ain home, so Miss Mavis, Ah res' mey case
Ah cuss wen Ah want an cou' tro' peasoup in yoh face
Call people *"no teet"* an' *"stuppidy,"* an arl dem ting so,
You ciarn do meh notin' 'cause Ah done is ah pappy show

'Cause mommy toh wok' an' Ah know she 'ain gon be back 'til sunset
So, Ah could bad talk jumbie fo'spite an' make dem obeah man sweat"

"Yes son, Ah don' see how yoh 'pout up yoh mout'
an' cussin' widout shame
ruinin' yoh nice mudda' reputation, ha good name"
bu' before deh boy cou' agin' run he foul mout' like ah man

Miss Mavis don' had ah long hard bostick waitin' in she han'

Yoh see, deh rude boy believe' that Miss Mavis was ole an' sick
Yes, meson, 'til he start' toh feel dem good ole-fashion bostick,
Amidst the scream there was a familiar voice heard at the boy's door:
"Miss Mavis, tis me, Ah home now, doan stap; please wail he tail some mo'!!"

Unbreakable Alliance

Caribbean sun does not burn me,
My friend needs a shield for protection,
I stare the Caribbean sun in the face
and boast of genes irrevocably altered
in order to withstand its scorching ways

Caribbean sun, like Tyson, throws its punches
of evil intentions,
But I stick to the brazen trade winds
seeking friendship with me,
caressing me from time to time
whispering to me: *"Defy the island's sun rays"*

Caribbean sun scares me at times, but I
continue to stare in arrogance because
I feel the gentle breeze on the
nape of my neck

Pouting sun hides its face in shame,
unable to force me to seek shelter,
and with this act of defiance,
I too am a contributor, like the ocean breezes
to the sun's deflated ego

Caribbean sun fails to burn me and
in a final gesture of mutual respect,
admits that it cannot
overcome the persistent trade winds
blowing indiscriminately
across my Virgin Islands land

Sea Wata' Treatment

He so[re]' foot miraculously heal' up
when he pu' it in deh sea
Sea Wata' curative powers legendary

Elders boast of "Sea Wata' " that strengthens bones
Eliminating back pains, improving muscle tone
Darg went deh sea deh odda day 'cause he owner say "*he mangy*"
Even carnt-swim ciat went deh Sea Wata' 'cause mangy darg bite he

Flu shot? we neva hea' 'bout dem 'ting back den in mey islans'
"*Soak yoh head chile, deh col' gon leave yoh whole body, man,*"
Trus' meh, partna,' it geh ah medicine chest in dem sea by deh rock
No matter wa' wrang wid yoh its proven formula duz wok like ah clock

Dem parents didn' like runnin' toh dem drugstore, no matter how close
Dem times wen deh lil ones dem had problems breathin' through deh nose
Instead dey use toh run toh dem beaches on our islands, even if was John
"Bruise"
Or sea wata' in Virgin Gorda, Tortola, Anegada, St John, Josh Von Dyke
or Santa Cruz

Migraine garn, bus' toe fix, so' foot arl heal-up,
broke han' o' foot mendin' real fas' an' ting'
Now Beego, yoh cou' jump in deh warm Sea Wata,
an' finally geh yoh nice lil' swim

Deh Rock-Stone Wars

Rock-stone throwing,
an art
when no truce could be reached,
armed camps displayed their
arsenals,
rock-stone designated toh "chap"
never toh maim,
rock-stone wid' mey name on it

not every one cou' fling ah good rock-stone
or could make it follow you 'roun ah buildin'
like wen ah boy name Mullet, or Crookéd,
'trow one dat follow' ah Housin' boy
'roun' buildin' 15 in Pearson Gardens
an' chap deh fellow

Dey say, boy take off runnin' den turn'
right de by ah lady we call' Miss B,
Mullet laughed: *"I ain even worried 'bout he
'causen I have ah rock-stone dat cou' fly like ah Trouchie
Le' 'im run, we gon see how fa' he will geh from me"*

Partna' make ah sharp turn up de by Elrod dem,
At dat point Mullet's adversary was unseen
But witnesses say the rock-stone stopped in the air
then suddenly made a sharp left, rock was lookin' mean

O.K. Ah confess dat me wern de, but Ah hea' dat night
deh head of dat Housin' boy was now clearly in full sight,
rock stone chap 'im, he went home cryin' toh he mudda'
"Yoh too disgustin" she scolded, while applyin' macuricome,
lil' salt an' wata, Epson Salt, inflamation bush an' cocoa butta'

Ole Years Comin'

Miss Sheila sen' meh toh buy two poun'
ah pig feet from La Lechonera shap
she 'gon cook callaloo,
"Ole Years comin', Marm?

—Yes, boy, run toh Lechonera an' buy deh ting
Mey neighbor dem waitin'
"Lechonera close, marm"
—Den go toh John Davis,
"He outta pig tail,"
—Go toh Denton, boy
"He garn chuch'"

—Go down Savan, yoh gon fin' it,
Ah want toh begin toh hot mey pot,
wen yoh go, tell dem Ah 'gon pay dem lata'
when Ah geh lil sometin',
tell dem Ah gon 'save dem lil' callaloo,
while yoh de, buy some brown suga',
lil' potato an' bread, ah poun' ah lard
tell dem Ah wan' toh trus' arl ah it

Befo' yoh go, stap in an tell yoh mudda' Ah sen' yoh
Hurry back, sonny, befo' deh rain come
Hurry back, boy, befo' de sun set
Doan play on de wharf yoh might fall in deh sea
Stay away from deh boathouse, doan go lookin' company

Doan go swimmin', Sonny, somebardy gon tell meh
Plus yoh don know dem shark an' barra dem doan play
Go an' come dereckly 'cause mey new gas stove duz cook good
Wen yoh geh back, if Ah 'ain heh, leave deh ting in front deh do'

But doan' stop toh play no marble, yoh tink Ah ain know yoh
Neighbor dem waitin,' dyin' foh' lil callaloo, lil' fellow
Hurry, go so come Ah tell yoh,' Ah really need dem pig feet, yoh hea'
Ah mus' have mey callaloo befo' deh start of DEH NEW YEAR

Darg So Mangy II

Mangy darg of deh Virgin Isluns use' toh have
He way way back then,
Not 'fraid ah no so-called masta',
'cause he 'ain had none,
Dat mangy darg of mey isluns

Mangy darg
King an' queen of our landscape,
Dem mangy darg use' toh play deady,
But bite yoh fo' spite, wen dey feel bored,
Dem Virgin Isluns mangy darg

Mangy darg in deh street
Mangy darg in dem alley
Coopin' yoh wen yoh goin' home,
Mangy darg on unauthorized patrol,
Mangy darg ask meh toh put 'im on ah leash
Ah respon': "*Mangy, yoh ain no frien ah mine,
Go 'mongst yoh sex, mangy one,
Ah ain goin' no place wid yoh in public*"

Neighbor trow' darg food toh
Mangy darg
Mangy darg wan' steak,
Chicken, fry' fish an' ting
While househol' back den
Rejoice' wid carn meal pap
Rice an' milk an' cream ah wheat

Mey cousin' Ellie in La Vallee
Trow bone toh mangy darg
Mangy darg trow it back,
Cousin' Hubert gi' he "DOG CHOW"
Upscale darg bran',
Mangy laugh' in he face sayin:
"Yoh gon eat it yo'self!"

Mangy darg in mey Grove Place yard
see cereal on deh menu an' rip it up wid he crookidy teet',
Deh mangy darg of the Virgin Isluns
Self-centered mangy ting
Spoil' by the populace,
Eatin he way tru every Big Yard
An' every islander's HEART

Crisis Of Identity

Who were those people?
I want to know
Did they run? Did they hide?
I need to know,
Who were my grandmothers'
grandmothers and grandfathers,
my grandfathers' grandfathers
and grandmothers?
I am dying to know,
thoughts of the ancestral line dominate
my mind,
Who created granny's great great
granny?
The thought is inebriating,
Intoxicants send me staggering
through the streets of
history's uneven roads

What did they look like?
like me?
Like my children?
Like my grandchildren?
Repository of the genetic markers?
Who were those people?
And who took them away on
the boats for tourists,
kind and benevolent travel agents
offering them an opportunity
of a lifetime

to see new places,
fun places,
        experience winter,
        snow for the first time
        learn new languages,
English, perhaps
        Dutch, perhaps
        Danish, No!

Travel agents with the
best itinerary,
Unbeatable Slogans:
        SEE THE WORLD FOR FREE,
        BASK IN THE SUN,
        IN THE CARIBBEAN SUN

Just who were those people?
I must know!

Legacy

My father's St. Croix
never abandoned me
never left me,
Some claimed that his
Grove Place did not belong
To my Granny, this
Nevisian born and raised,
Matriarch of the St. Croix
And St. Thomas clan,
But Grove and Frederiksted
Denied the claim
Giving my granny full
Status as Grovian and
A product of Wes' End,
Others asserted that
Auntie dem, and uncle should
Claim their space in Nevis,
And not St. Croix,
Not being born in that
Great land,
But MY St. Croix rejected that,
adopting Granny
And hers, and mine,
As they themselves adopted Cruz, Ay Ay,
The land of my father,
Who traced his roots to the
Same Gingerland space as
Did mey Granny,
Actions that continuously

Transform me in ways
Unclear to myself
Or to the detractors
Who try to unhinge me from
My Crucian and Nevisian self!

Mangy Revisited: Mey Bes' Frien'
(for Glen Kwabena Davis)

Deh mangy one
Star protagonist of our land
Skinnin' up he wolf-like face
Saliva drippin,' signal of
Greed 'cause he want toh bite
All in sight

Ole' mangy self
He tink he betta' dan we
Showin arf, rollin' 'roun' in dut
Swattin' flea, like only he know toh do da'

But Ah still admire 'im
Our famous mangy darg
Dat deserve he rightful place
Wid deh famous V.I. characters
Wid dem mangoose an' ting'
Dem guana
Dem lizard an' wood slaves
Deh gongolo dem

Dese 'ain geh notin' on mey
Lazy, wutless fellow citizen
Mey good fo' notin mangy darg frien'

Forget deh lice an' ting
On he rough-dry back,
Mangy is really good company

Lazily positioned in one ah dem
Big Yard in our V.I.,
Minin' he own business

Ah tell ah yoh one ting,
Bring back mey mangy darg,
Ah miss he funny face
Repulsive lookin' self,
Call meh crazy
But Ah use toh like seein' deh
Scaly one roamin' our isluns,
Ah wan' toh lime wid deh
Famous mangy one,
Jus' one mo' time!!

Obeah Man Doan' Tell Untrut'
(For Torian "Muscles" Martin/Ladell and LaSheryl Perez)

Obeah man tell me someting ah fin' hard toh believe
Bu' how he use' toh wok back in deh Garden of Eden,
Keepin' company wid deh fus parents, Adam an' Eve
Some stuieppidness like he have power jus' like dem Diety

Ah wuz tinkin' dat maybe dat fella believe Ah crazy
Makin' up arl kind ah strange stories toh tell me,
But I know dat no obeah man was present aroun' creation time
Mey gran'parents ha' don' tell me such thought is ah crime

"Ah tarkin' deh trut,' " obeah man said toh meh dat day
"Any action yoh need done, come toh me, yoh doan have toh pray
'Cause Ah duz fix up arl kin ah love relationship an' ting
Come toh me an' Ah will guarantee yoh dat coveted weddin' ring

Ah duz fix money problems, correct behavior of children, mey frien'
We obeah man duz cause pain an' sufferin' toh immediately en'"
Ah look in obeah man eyes and scream out, "*Man, dat's ah lie*"
"*Dat's hut'ful words*," Obeah man said, "*yoh makin' meh cry*"

"Sayin' bu' how Ah duz lie, toh you may seem very cute
Bu' Ah prefer if yoh simply say, '*Obeah fella, yoh untrut!*'
Bu' Ah say toh you go check out deh Obeah man history
Yoh gon fine' out dat deh obeah man is ah man of mystery

People fear us fo' no reason—but we on deh people dem side,
Yet some wen dey see meh, duz take off runnin, an' hide,
See meh as ah public servant, doin' good, protectin' mey folk

130

Ah doan' waste time, compado, Ah doan fool aroun' an' joke

Ah heh toh tell mey story, Ah want yoh toh geh use toh it now,
We obeah man duz always manage toh survive some kina how,
Bu' wen yoh slanda mey good name Ah gotta bring ah law suit
'Causen Ah don' tell yoh meson, Obeah man doan tell no untrut!"

Caregivers
(Dr. Paget henry)

Auntie Telma from St John's Antigua
Generous kind, selfless lady,
Aunt Telma renamed
In St. Thomas, maybe Miss Celes',
Miss Sella, Miss Lopie
The Aunt Telma's of our islands,
West Indian heroines
Giving, and not asking for rewards,
Sacrificing
Seeking no recompense
Nothing in return for
Their contributions to the welfare
Of theirs and those not theirs,
Because all belong to them,
All are theirs
Aunt Telma operating in another's behalf,
Knowing or not knowing her
Beneficiary irrelevant,
Not at all pertinent
In order to feed,
Clothe
Give that last cent,
Aunt Telma from St. John Antigua
Was from St. John, Virgin Islands
From St Croix, Nevis and St. Kitts,
I saw Aunt Telma in Tortola giving her all
To those in need
I recognize her because she looked

Exactly like Miss Maggie from Virgin Gorda,
Like mey auntie dem in Grove, Fredriksted, La Vallee
Aunt Telma's identical twin lives
In Barbados and Tobago,
I know them well,
I met them all,
And my mind still
Depends on them to lead,
As I try to master and apply those lessons
Taught for free by
Auntie Telma in her
Characteristic unassuming demeanor
Of love for her sister and
Brother islander
In a way only the Auntie Telmas can deliver
That Antiguan woman setting the
Tone of generosity and
goodness

Jumbie Altercation

Two Jumbie pose' off in front of each other one dreary V.I. day
"Go ahead" said Jumbie One "now lemme hea' wa yoh geh toh say"
"Ah mo' jumbie dan you, partna'," screamed out Jumbie Two,
"Wa yoh jus' say toh meh," said Jumbie One, "jus' 'ain true"

'Cause Ah duz roam deh graveyard dem mo' hours dan you
While yoh sleep, Ah duz patrol deh graveyard tru' an' tru"
"O.K" said Jumbie Two, "but Ah know everybody dat live heh by name
An' you 'ain know not one, boy, dat is really such ah terrible shame."

"Meet me lata, Jumbie Two, an' let's finally settle dis score
'Cause wen Ah talk toh you Ah duz geh angry more an' more,"
"Well, let's meet down by arm ting' kenip tree" said Jumbie Two
"No, no" complain' Jumbie One, "man, dem ting' too sour fo tru"

"Den meet meh ova' de by Wa' He Name dem mango tree"
"No, too much Jumbie out de dat Ah doan want toh see,
'Cause dey now geh arl kin' ah graveyard out ova' da side
Please understan' Ah have toh maintain some kin-ah pride"

"Yoh makin' all kine-ah excuse, look like yoh scared ah me,"
Screamed out Jumbie Two, now laughin' and gigglin' so silly,
Said Jumbie One, "Me' ain 'fraid ah notin,' no jumbie badda' dan me
Ah duz battle 'guana in deh bush an' even dem shark in deh deep sea"

"Come on, coward Jumbie, decide if we gon have dis fight at midnight,"
"No, Ah heh toh confess toh yoh," said Jumbie Two, "it's only right
To tell deh trut, arl dat runnin' mey mout' Ah had was only big tark
The real trut' is, jumbie frien', yoh jumbie partna' 'fraid ah deh dark!!"

134

Do Foh Do

Watch 'im good, wid eagle eyes, mey frien'
Den scrutinize every single move,
Doan be fool by dat smile, meson
He geh ah lot he wan toh prove

Ah say watch him good,
Keep 'im in yoh sight
Yoh mus' resis' he evil,
Every day, every night

Foh vengeance is *not* yours
So say dat very good Book
So every move partna' make
Yoh betta' take ah close look

Toh see if frogs an' lizards
Duz live full time in he house
If in it mongoose an guana
Duz play eveyday wid mouse

If he duz eat corn pork an' peas soup
An wash it arl down wid maubi
If he main bath of deh day
Duz be in the Caribbean Sea

Be ready toh match every step he take
Every tricky plan, any move he make,
An deh bush he bunnin' if it smell like bittah weed
Doan worry frien' jus' start toh plant yoh own seed

So dat wen eveyting tun' very dreary an' dark
Yoh don ready, yoh woan even have toh tark
Jus' tun yoh back toh he shoutin' he name like yoh doan care
Victory is yours, Secko, 'cause do *foh do ain no obeah*

Identity Riddle Unsolved

Who were those passengers?
and those before them who sailed the
Ocean blue seeking their fortune
in so-called" *civilized* zones that promised
To bring them over to
Civility?
Who were those people?
Waving to onlookers on their shores,
Waving to them, saying "goodbye,
Until we meet again,"
Anxiously waiting to meet the
Welcoming committee on the other side?
Journeys on the seas,
Upper deck closed,
But unlimited space below,
In that place with NO SPACE,
Who were those people?
Awaiting room service in the
Space so
Graciously reserved for them,
RESERVATION CONFIRMED
TO THE VIRGIN ISLANDS!
Who were they?
      I really must know!

Fraidy Cat

So Boysie convinced me that Ah cou'
beat Waldron
for that reason I walked up to his gate,
followed by an entourage of boys,
secretly, I wondered if this fella
cou' seal my fate

then Boysie call' Waldron
"You come outside right away"
As I heard those words thought I:
"Wa' Waldron gon do toh meh today?"

Really, I didn't know this boy Waldron
Only heard how much this fellow could fight
But my supporters told me that I had a much better right

In the direction of Logan Church we headed, the protagonist
and coaches, a side show
I kept on telling myself, *"Meson, Ah cou' beat him, yoh know"*

My brother, was older an' wiser, dat was a plus
"Yoh cou' beat Waldron," said he, "hit him fus"
But soon Waldron was standing out in the yard
Thought I, *"Dat Waldron fellow look real hard"*

"Hit him fus" shouted my brother, Reovan, also named Cordell
"Bus him ah hard thump, put on ah neck hold, push him 'gainst deh well"

Then it came to my mind, "Logan Church carn save meh
From a boy so strong
Muscles bulging, reach so long,"
"Brudda," said I, "me ain wan' notin' wid this boy Waldron today"
"Doan' be ah fraidy cat" said my brother, "doan' talk dat way"

"Look heh, Big brudda' an' Boysie, Ah doan care wa' ah yoh say,
Ah see dat Waldron boy is anxious to make me cry in some way"
And since deh lil' Savan Church next toh he house couldn' save me if Ah cry,
Widout tinkin', Ah bid mey adversary and mey coaches dem, GOODBYE!!!

Funny-Up Lizard

But woodslave,
Way pa' yoh garn?
I ain see yoh since
Yoh crawled all over
Our dwelling in Savan,
Yoh creepy self
Woodslave, Ah didn' min'
Watchin deh brown lizard,
but you scared me with yoh
prehistoric look,
Ah sorry, yoh jus' look funny-up,
Woodslave, Ah carn call yoh frien',
Wen Ah tink' 'bout yoh
Ah duz shut mey eyes dem tight
Trying toh erase yoh from mey mind's register
Ah carn stan' dem eyes,
dat crazy tail
dat dragon look

Ah even ain sure if yoh duz bite people
Cause Ah ain see no teet' atarl
In yoh mout,
Yoh no-teet self!
You losin' yoh pulls,
Woodslave
mongoose an' guana geh
mo' fame dan you,
look like dey heh toh stay,
reassert yoh self

an' figure dis ting out,
yoh use' toh give me the creeps,
but partna' dis time
wen yoh come back,
doan leh dat mangy darg
replace yoh,
wid he less man self,
Woodslave,
Wey yoh be?
Ah say,
Wey pa' yoh garn?

Ah Wuz De
(For MARY, I STILL THINK ABOUT YOU)

Mary lost her arm, up there in a church
in Savan
I was de!
I really wish that instead of cussin' dat chile
Deh chuch people dem had prayed,
She wuz jus' ah little guirl, doin' no harm
Why such a reaction, why wasn't the congregation alarmed?

Little Mary, with other Savaneros at play
Didn't expect that kind of reception that day
Anguish, pain, seen in that little angel's face
The apathy shown by the church was truly a disgrace,
an innocent being lost her arm in the 1950's, one summer's night
I was de,
now bearing witness
that tragedy was not handled right!
Mary lost her arm, up there in
a church
in Savan
It is true,
I was de!

Truchie Dem Garn

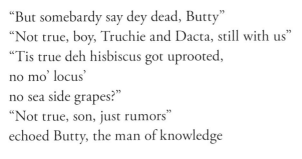

Tis true deh truchie dem dead?
And deh Dacta' bird dem?
Must be true 'cause Ah 'ain seein' none
Ah once asked Butty, the teller of tales,
He said, "They are still around"

"But somebardy say dey dead, Butty"
"Not true, boy, Truchie and Dacta, still with us"
"Tis true deh hisbiscus got uprooted,
no mo' locus'
no sea side grapes?"
"Not true, son, just rumors"
echoed Butty, the man of knowledge

"And dem dates by deh big Post Office,
Dey rotten?"
"No, just hearsay"
"So wey deh hag plum dem, Butty?
Deh marmey?"
"Up in the bushes, boy"
"Ah scared ah stinga-nettle"
"Ah 'fraid kasha"
"There is no kasha, no stinga nettle"
the poet, possible descendant of
the Ashantis said,
"They are all buried in the vicinity
of the houses of cement"
"But Butty
—not deh same houses dat replaced

deh locus'
dem plums
deh dates?
So dat's why deh truchie and Dacta'
dem garn?"
"Too painful to discuss,
too painful to contemplate," moaned the
reciter of verses and preserver of
West Indian and Virgin Islands culture
looking sadly at the
concrete jungle
in the distance

Wey Deh Congo Dem?

Some Housin' boys rock some congo in deh sea
I ain' went too close because no congo 'gon bite me

Everyday on deh bay was jelly fish we called sea moon,
also barra,' sting-ah ray and shark, ova' in Pantoom
We use' toh kill soldier crab dat neva' trouble we
Bus' up sea-egg, trow rock-stone at schools ah fish in deh sea

Dem boy use' toh hunt Dacta' and Trouchie, Ah neva know why
Toh tell deh trut' Ah ha' rather see dem bird fly high up de in deh sky

But dem Woodslave an' Mangy Darg an' so, Ah really coun' stan'
I ha' hate dem gongolo even though I used toh hol' dem in mey han'

Dem santapee were numerous in Savan undah our wood house
Dey cohabited with spider, roach and ah bunch ah nasty mouse

Now Ah doan see dem congo, or maybe dey duz run from me,
Look like deh gongolo dem die out, also dem funny-up santapee

Wey dem sting ah ray garn and dem sea egg, soldier crab and so?
Well, meson, Ah really doan' see none ah dem ting so no mo!

The Real Danjah

Runnin' out of deh Western Cemetery
ah fall in deh big gut
Ah geh ah bonkonko,
Bu' toh tell deh trut', 'tain really 'hut

I 'ain know why Ah wuz runnin' so crazy dat night
No jumbie nor obeah man, no Cow Foot woman in sight,
Green Face man dey say was home, not even studyin' me
Lata' Ah hea' he wuz jumpin' from limb toh limb in some tree

Mey mudda want toh know why Ah wuz down in deh buryin' groun' dat
hour
She had sen' me toh deh shap, Ah went slingarin' an' clean forget she flour
Playin' too larng, ah notice' afterward dat Mr. Denton shop don close
So Ah wuz 'fraid toh go home 'cause Ah know Ah gon eat mo' blows

Waitin' fo' mey mudda toh fall asleep befo' ah return' home
Ah had the bright idea toh pick ah bunch ah tarmon' arl alone
Somebardy had tell me 'bout dis sweet tree in deh graveyard
So Ah decide toh walk down de by meyself, feelin' Ah was bad

Ah climb' one tarmon tree and pick' ah lot of deh bitta-sweet fruit
Tinkin' toh meyself: *"Some fo' mommy, dat's easier than tellin' deh trut'*
Dat Ah didn' buy her flour dat she ha' need right away in order toh bake
Deh dumbread wid fish and some nice tastin' Virgin Islands johnnycake"

Goin' back up deh tree again, Ah hea' dis strange, loud soun'
Ah stop in deh middle of mey climb, from fright, start toh look aroun'
Ah ain see notin', partna', notin' atarl, no Jumbie eye,

Jus' ah clear night regular beautiful Virgin Islands sky

Ah start' toh relax, feelin' right at home an' very well at ease
Den Ah see two man playin' domino and jus' shootin' deh breeze
Dey was watchin' me kina ah hard, yoh know, but Ah 'ain say ah word,
Den one ah dem den say sometin' strange 'bout people born wid ah cord,

Now since Ah was so young an' didn' quite grasp tings like dat
Ah tell meyself, "*Look, yoh betta, get out ah heh, boy, SCIAT!*"
Wen Ah look' again deh two man dem wuz don' garn,
I know den Ah wouldn' be in dat place fo' too larng,

So Ah grab' mey tarmon dem, some fo' mey mudda,' and break like ah jet,
Listen Compado, believe me Ah neva' run so fas' in mey whole life yet
Ah forget deh gut was close toh deh wall, boy, Ah fall an' nearly geh mey
deat' dat night
But tis tinkin' 'bout mey mudda at de do' wid ah broad belt make meh
fall from fright!

Friendship Housin'* Style
(Dedicated to the memory of Lionel "Frako" Farrington)

Deh day of dey fus' meetin'
Tony "Maltin" White wid he fancy
Wheelbarrow, wid its tinin fenders
An' modern horn,
Run ova' Frako Farrington kite,
He favorite Spanish**
Frako took exception to this willful act
Daring Maggie son to repeat his
Act of defiance,
So toh prove heself ah true housin' boy,
Maltin crush frako Spanish, boastin:
"See Ah do it again, wa yoh gon do?"
Fisticuffs flyin on dat summer day in 1955,
Victory claimed by frako fo' Miss Telma,
Maggie boy boasted of Frako's defeat
Miss Telma son and Maggie own, rootin' in
Deh grass in Pearson Gardens,
Like so many odda' housin' boys, befo' an afta',
Wreslin', neckhol', scissors an' ting,
Learnin' toh defend themselves, but unaware of the
Skills, action on deh groun'
De by Miss Becca,
By Miss Becca New Road,
sweet scent of cakes an' tarts,
Maltin tell he brodda he beat up dis boy,
Ah housin' fella' name' Frako,
Frako brudda Roland Bloat announce'
His broudda victorious escapade,

But only one constant truth in the
Multiple versions:
Maltin an' Frako remain 'bes' ah friends
'Til July 27, 2014
Wen Frako fo' mis telma,
Still clamin' victory ova' Maltin,
bid farewell
To Tony fo' Maggie an' arl he housin
Boy *dem*

*In the 1950's, 60's, 70's, & 80's *this was the common designation for* Paul M Pearson Gardens in St. Thomas, Virgin Islands. Those who lived there during those years still use this term. Our dear friend, Lionel "Frako" Farrington, "housin boy," died on July 27, 2014 in New York

**A special type of kite designed by island children to take advantage of prevailing winds

Deh Real Olympics
(For Tin Tin/ Sharon "Blue" Smalls/ Ruby D./Guirlie)

Dem housin boys an' guirls use' toh skate like pros
Glitterin Fly Away skates*, favorite Christmas gift
Fo' dem housin chiren
No Chicago Roller Skates fo' dem Pearson Gardens
Athletes zoomin' down Watafront,
Challengin' the island's few cars,
Dem housin chiren
Blazin' on dem sidewalks in Housin'
Bunnin' off adults, but neva' collidin'
Wid dem
Guirlie an' Blue dem, Ruby too
Diamond wid he unique eagle move,
Wid he signature towel 'roun' he neck,
Smooth Diamond,
Challenged by Teddy an' dem
Fordy an' Bayie Sela, Myie
Aubrey V.
Maybe "V' for velocity!
Speeding, Spinnin', jumpin',
Flash an' dem,
Sasso too,
Bobby wid he booths
Skate,
deh only housin' boy wid lace' up shoes,
Housin' boys an' guirls mashin' up concrete
Jus' from speed,
Tin Tin an dem guirls showin' dem housin boys
A ting o' two,
Housin boys dem doin' 360 on deh

150

Basketball court of juvenile fun,
Housin' boys playin 3 on 3 wid skates
Housin' guirls matchin dem,
Fly Away, main transportation
To La Lechonera, 'Potechiary
To Deh Markit

To buy tings fo our mammies,
Dem who use toh pay fo' dem
Cherished and treasured
Fly Aways,
The vehicles mastered by dem
Housin' chiren, together frolickin'
Havin fun
Enjoyin' each other,
Lovin one another
Dem housin sports stars wid
Deh hot wheels
Dem jet wheels
Dem Fly Away roller skates
Conduit toh everlastin' friendship,
Bonds of brotherhood
Sisterhood
Cemented eternally by
The shiny metal skates
Owned and
Operated by dem
Masters of balance,
Agility,
Coordination,
Style
An' genuine solidarity

*speedy skates preferred by the children of Pearson Gardens in the 50's,
60's, 70's

Yoh Good Shoes

School shoes
chuch shoes
fit for true worshipers of faith,
No school shoes this day,
Tomorrow is school
doan put on deh good shoes now,
chuch' shoes toh put away,
bus toe afta' school
bus mey toe on ah rock-stone down
on deh bayside
ah fin' some brown papah on deh groun'
an' wrap mey big toe,
limpin' home, ah trow
some well wata on it,
nail chook, day befo,
step' on ah rusty nail
'roun' deh rocks, pickin' welks,
no tetanus shot
pu' iodine on deh ting
soak in deh bay right by Housin',
dry off wid deh bay side leaves
ready toh put on dem chuch shoes
soon,
chuch Sunday!

Caribbean Acrobatics

Seagulls charging noisily in the Caribbean
skies,
preys marked, or unmarked,
The patient gulls head downward,
Their symmetric skyward trail
The envy of the pigeons peering upward
from their secure spot
on the sand,
Having wandered there to pick the residues
of beings,
daily visitors to their place of worship under the sun,
island pigeons,
distracted constantly
by the gulls of precision in
aerial exhibitions,
acrobatic ostentatious shows
done unabashedly above the heads of
doting pigeons not at all oblivious
to the dynamics of the world above
detached from theirs below,
the world high above the
gradually eroding sand on the
beach at the foot of enormous
idle boulders of the sea

New Bully

Kiat dem doan sleep in mey house no mo'
dey 'fraid dem rat, now so big,
Chemical laden rodent
Big fo' spite, caravan of nibbly
freaks
carrying furniture upon their backs,
poison doan wok,
venom laced peanut butter tastes good
What a meal!

Kiat 'fraid mouse
what ah mix-up!!
In this neighborhood nobardy
duz see kiat,
Rat eat dem,
Dine on dem one Thanksgiving Day,
Spit out deh bones down de
by Glass bottle Alley,
some'ting Gade

Rat Dem boast of Thanksgiving feast,
kiat soup next day
kiat sandwich
kiat pie
Ah hea' dem kiat now keepin' deh safe distance,
'Cause dem pumped up modernized, chemicalized
rats doan play, meson,
Next on deh menu
–Deh mangy darg dem of
the Virgin Islands!

Miss Sela Boy

Garn minin' dis boy, Bayie Sela
an' forge' in one day toh Hass Race:
Granslam' versus Celosa,
Black Beauty 'gainst anodda horse,
Mey partna' strategy backfire',
Plan doomed toh fail from deh start

Walk' tru High School gate
Hike' up dat steep hill
Walk east 'til yoh geh toh deh track,
Ah garn minin' Bayie fo' Miss Sela,
Kasha
ketch & keep
dem hook' me,
sting-ah-nettle bump' up mey skin,
mosquitos an' ting'
Even san' fly in deh bush,
Neva' hea' wus!

But we wan' toh see deh race dem,
Especially las' race, feature race:
Celosa versus Grandslam,
Ah sneak' with Bayie Sela 'cross deh
steep hill wey de kasha dem was,
no mango
no kennip
no tarmon
Man so hungry!

Kasha still in our foot
we reach' Lockhart track,
Horse race don ova'
Face and foot bump up,
fo' notin',
minin' dat Bayie Sela!

Jus' He An' Me

Ah recognize he face wen he sit' down by me
Ah ha meet 'im befo' undah ah tiny sour sap tree
Ah wuzn' 'fraid atarl of dem big piercin' eyes
Though yoh might tink mey words ah bunch ah lies

He wuz tryin' toh geh meh toh follow 'im aroun'
But Ah didn' say yes, o no, didn' make ah soun'
Arl Ah cou feel was sometin' strange in deh air
Dis partna' next toh meh now givin' meh much toh fear

"*Strike up ah conversashun wid deh strange man,*" Ah start toh tink,
It was den he sen' meh ah signal, ah lazy funny-up wink
Ah coun' figure out fo' sure wa wuz he game,
No matter wa' it wuz, it was scary arl deh same

Ah scrutinize deh fella unda dat lil' beat up tree dat day,
To my reader, the following is the only thing I will say:
"Deh fella look' like ah 'para' man, so ting-up an' so,
Betta' geh some sour sap now fo' mey mudda, den go"

Ah neva' trus' dem de wid deh face arl ben' up an' ting
So Ah was pretendin' toh be happy, start toh whistle an' den sing
Deh half dead man skin-up he face jus' like dem ram ciat,
He face look so bad like the joinin' of ah rodent wid ah bat

Den he keep gigglin' so stuiepidy an' laughin' fo' spite
Meh po' heart wuz failin' from dis melee an' fright
I was worried how dis strange bein' jus' keep on lookin' at me
So Ah gather deh fruits dem quick 'cause it was time toh flee!

Walkin' Truck

(Kwame Motilewa)

Tam truck was so slow,
dem boy use' toh give him start,
Tam wid he
"sure lif'" truck,
Mr. Tam
wid he pick-up
strainin' toh climb Raphune hill,
but, he always gave you ah ride,
or,
anyway,
eveyone always jump' on the
slowes' movin' truck on St
Thomas,
Dis vehicle belongin'
toh Tam,
Wayne, o' Ivis
Darwin dem
Charles dem
Clifford,
Tito dem,
Tam's truck daily leadin' the young
boys to their destination—
kennip trees,
mango trees
suga' apple, mesple, guava,
in the COUNTRY,
Tam's *putt putt* knew where they were,
the driver was taken there too,

by the truck with a sense
of direction,
Mr. Tam, an' he slow truck, even
José, Quilly, and Docka,
the slowes' boys in
Housin' use' toh race and win,
yes, they would beat
Tam and he truck,
a truck etched forever in the minds
of dem housin' boys,
who now smile wen dey remember
the slowes' movin' vehicle on
deh rock,
But, dat sure ride to country!

'Tis True, Ask Crimmo

(for Melvin "Crimmo" Testamark)

Believe me, I confirm that the following story is one hundred percent true,
Dis fellow hungrily sat down at our small eatin' table in Housin', Blg 22,
Way Back in '58 he ask' meh one day *"Meson wa' yoh mudda cook?"*
Ah tell him; deh boy rush' toh mey mudda' house wid he hungry look

He was waitin' at deh eatin' table, mout' watery from anticipation,
He face was wet from hunger pang, and an' jus' en'less perspiration,
Look like he coun' wait a secon' toh sink he teet' in mey mudda' food,
Man, deh boy so hungry he was don' aready in ah very nasty mood

Said the fellow: *"Bring deh food, Blanco, bring deh chow right now,*
Look, Ah doan need no vegetable, Ah cou' eat dat ting' anyhow,"
So Ah start' toh hurry up 'cause Ah want toh bring mey frien' deh ting
'Cause judgin' from deh look on he face, dis housin' boy was starvin'

So then bellowed he: *"Boy dat plate look so beautiful, so nice*
Bu' wait, Secko, it look like it only geh in it ah bunch white rice,
Wa' wrang wid yoh, Blanco, dis ain' no food fo' ah king,
Dis saucer from your mudda' sho' case ain geh no sal'ting"

"Wey deh mutton," Melvin-Crimmo' whine,' *"dat yoh say Miss Maggie prepare'"*
"Crimmo, partna', you need toh go home an' clean deh wax real good from yoh ear
'Cause Ah don tell yoh already, in fact, Ah know Ah tell yoh much mo' dan twice
NOT that Mammy cook rice wid **MUTTON**, Ah say she cook' **NOTIN'** AN' RICE!"

My Original Inner Truths

—A lead singer may have the voice of a nightingale, converted to that of an owl without his/her backup chorus

—Acknowledge those who touch your hand, cherish those who touch your heart

—Allow no one to define the parameters of your success through concocted notions of who you are or should be

—Arrogance inevitably breeds complacency, itself a blueprint for failure

—Audacity may at times disguise itself as assertiveness

—Believe in yourself, but do not become stifled by vanity

—Complacency will asphyxiate and stagnate you

—Compromise your integrity and begin the first step towards self-destruction

—Conceding your lack of knowledge is the first step toward a solid education

—Dig deep into yourself and witness possibilities springing forth from the well

—Do not be complicit in your own downfall

—Do not become intoxicated by the fumes of your success

—Don't be strangled by the urge to compete against others, challenge yourself, the most formidable competitor

—Don't dream of dreamers dreaming you

—Don't dwell on probabilities, but instead invest in the limitless possibilities

—Don't live trying to please your loved ones, but to better their lot

—Dwell on the past and be strangled by its tentacles of stagnation

—Educate yourself before you dare to assume the education of others

—Education begins within you

—Even the most dreaded curve in the road in the road of life, can lead you to a place where your dreams will be fulfilled

—Fail to recognize who you are and stumble on yourself in the darkness

—Faith ceases to be thus when effort and application reveal themselves
—Faith must not yield to pragmatism
—He/she who boasts of modesty tacitly admits arrogance
—He/she who shelters knowledge spreads ignorance
—Honor your family and in the process bring honor to yourself
—If you believe that education begins in the classroom, you have already begun the process of miseducation
—Inspire one person, then stand back and witness the magic of permutation at work
—Learn who you are by exploring the unchartered dimensions of yourself
—Listening is the centerpiece of the art of meaningful communication
—Lower the sound of arrogance to truly hear yourself
—Nature is recalling its own
—No truth greater than that which awakens your conscience
—One's greatest strength may well be the acknowledgment of his/her weaknesses
—Opportunity may not necessarily identify itself, introduce yourself to it
—Seek advice but ultimately listen to the voice from within
—Silence yourself before silencing others
—Silence yourself in order to hear yourself
—Tell who you are, less through words, but by the blueprint of your actions
—The first step of many steps may be unrecorded but it is the base for the later more heralded ones
—The individual who believes that he/she is "self-made" is delusional
—The loudest voice in the choir is not necessarily the best
—The most brilliant individual may well be she/he who brings out the brilliance in others
—The most deadly, ghastly fear, is the fear of oneself
—The only way to avert the atrocities of the past is to subvert the ideological traps securely set in history
—The stranger you fear may be yourself
—The suffering independent nation may well be in better shape than the overly dependent thriving state
—There is no such thing as a solo act
—Treat me royally and receive my gratitude, treat me fairly earn my respect

—Trust those who have proven their love through action; eye suspiciously those who only boast of it

—Wealth is defined as the reservoir of unbridled humanity embedded in your soul

—What is knowledge but the willingness to concede the lack of it?

—What is the past if not a barometer of the future?

—When the voice of reason and rationality is ignored, the door of anarchy and chaos automatically swings wide open

—Who are we? Coming from others who come from elsewhere who are coming from others coming from elsewhere?

—Your greatest benefits may well be those done for others

—Your mother, though gone, still is the rudder of the ship on this journey

—Your quest to comprehend the world must begin with your resolve to know yourself

===
===

Printed in the United States
By Bookmasters